WHAT PEOPLE ARE S

ARE YOU HAP

"Here's some real news – a self-help book that actually gives you some help! It doesn't make you think that you are doing EVERY-THING wrong, but shows you how you can – with simple adjustments in your way of thinking – make everything (in life) much easier for yourself. At the same time, the book is filled with easy-to-understand case stories so you better understand Barbara Berger's wise points. The book ends with 10 simple exercises that are designed to help you change your view of life. And Berger isn't even holy... clearly a MUST read!"
Cosmopolitan magazine

"Feeling blue and grumpy has long been on its way out – and it's in to be happy. And now help is on the way in Barbara Berger's new self-help book *Are You Happy Now?* The book is divided into 10 sections, each of which points to an important step along the way to a happier and more authentic life. The book ends with a series of exercises to achieve this. Very practical. The book is easy to read and gives easy-to-understand guidance in positive thinking. The book will surely give people who are worried about life a real 'aha' experience."
Femina magazine

"The point is that it's not outer circumstances that make us happy and this book gives us 10 practical suggestions as to how we can use this understanding in our daily lives."
Berlingske Tidende (Denmark's biggest newspaper)

Are You Happy Now? was the book-of-the-month selection. "We've had great success with Barbara Berger's books in the book club over the years and I can promise you that *Are You Happy Now?* is the most interesting and easy-to-read book Barbara has ever written. The title is a provocative question that really makes you think. I wish that I always jumped out of the bed in the morning with a smile on my lips, but the truth is I don't. But with Barbara's 10 Ways (which are based on her life's wisdom both as a private person and as a spiritual seeker), it really is easier. I had so many 'aha' experiences when I read Barbara's many examples – and by using her practical tools, I really am starting to think differently. Because whether we are happy or unhappy all depends on our thoughts. Try Barbara's 10 Ways and watch how happiness comes pouring in!!"

Agneta Gynning, Editor in Chief Livsenergi Book Club (Sweden)

Are You HappyNow?

10 Ways to Live a Happy Life

Other books by Barbara Berger

The Road to Power
Fast Food for the Soul

The Road to Power 2
More Fast Food for the Soul

Gateway to Grace
Barbara Berger's Guide to User-Friendly Meditation

Mental Technology (The 10 Mental Laws)
Software for Your Hardware

The Spiritual Pathway
A Guide to the Joys of Awakening and Soul Evolution

The Adventures of Pebble Beach
Single for the Second Time

The Awakening Human Being
A Guide to the Power of Mind (with Tim Ray)

Sane Self Talk
Cultivating the Voice of Sanity Within

Are You HappyNow?

10 Ways to Live a Happy Life

Barbara Berger

BOOKS

Winchester, UK
Washington, USA

First published by O-Books, 2013
O-Books is an imprint of John Hunt Publishing Ltd., Laurel House, Station Approach,
Alresford, Hants, SO24 9JH, UK
office1@jhpbooks.net
www.johnhuntpublishing.com

For distributor details and how to order please visit the 'Ordering' section on our website.

Text copyright: Barbara Weitzen Berger 2006

ISBN: 978 1 78279 201 7

A CIP catalogue record for this book is available from the British Library.

Design: Lee Nash
Cover photo: Søren Solkaer Starbird

Printed and bound by CPI Group (UK) Ltd, Croydon, CR0 4YY

We operate a distinctive and ethical publishing philosophy in all
areas of our business, from our global network of authors to
production and worldwide distribution.

CONTENTS

> **The number 1 cause of suffering and unhappiness is
> wanting life to be something it's not.**

> **The number 2 cause of suffering and unhappiness is
> wanting what you don't have.**

> **The number 3 cause of suffering and unhappiness is
> not communicating honestly with yourself.**

> **The number 4 cause of suffering and unhappiness
> are the scary stories you tell yourself
> about life and the world.**

> **The number 9 cause of suffering and unhappiness is wanting absolute satisfaction from relative experiences.**

> **The number 10 cause of suffering and unhappiness is believing we become nothing.**

Introduction

This book came about when I was lying on my sofa one afternoon thinking to myself... "OK Barbara, now that you've been through so much and are getting older, what do you need to remember to live a happy life? If you would sum it all up, what would it be? What do you need to know to get you through the rest of your life in a better way?"

So I wrote this list.

I wrote down the points that I thought were important. Just to see if I could sum it up for myself. And then I started writing down why I thought each of these points was important – again just to explain it to myself. I thought if I could explain it to myself then maybe I would remember the points better. And then maybe I'd be able to live the remainder of my life a little more wisely, a little more peacefully, a little more happily.

Because you see, looking back, I could see how much of my life I spent worrying about stuff or being nervous and insecure about stuff or not really enjoying the fullness and richness of my life. I had to admit that to myself. Because it seemed to me – in retrospect – that even though I've had a wonderful, exciting life, I was often worried about something or afraid of something or anxious about something. And look what happened! I got here anyway. Despite all the worries! Somehow I made it to today. I might not be able to tell you exactly how, but here I am anyway. Sitting right here in front of my computer. Maybe a bit worse for wear, but sitting here just the same! So what did I learn from all of this?

In other words, what does it take to live a happy life?

This is what I've found out so far – and am trying to live.

Maybe it can help you too!

> Where's the proof?
> When I do the things in this book, I feel happy!

The 10 ways:
Accept what is
Want what you have
Be honest with yourself
Investigate your stories
Mind your own business
Follow your passion and accept the consequences
Do the right thing and accept the consequences
Deal with what is in front of you and forget the rest
Know what is what
Learn to see beyond impermanence

Accept what is

The number 1 cause of suffering and unhappiness is wanting life to be something it's not.

This basically is our main problem. We want life to be something it's not. We want the impossible.

Just think about it.

Don't you want the impossible? Like living forever in this body? Don't you want that? And don't you want to feel good all the time, and look great, and be in control too? And don't you want to be strong and healthy and never get sick or tired or be in pain? And wouldn't you like to succeed at everything you do? And have everyone love and respect you no matter what? And wouldn't you like to... Well yes, the list is rather long when you think about it, isn't it?

But the reality is that life isn't like that. Do you know anyone who has lived forever and never died? Or someone who never got sick and never grew old? Probably not because the reality is that there is no one. The reality is that bodies come and go and that they break down, grow old and die. That's just the way it is.

And as for love and approval, the reality is people don't love and approve of us all the time no matter what we do, and we often don't succeed at what we're doing even if we try really hard. That's just the way it is.

In fact, in the life most of us are living, things just happen. Events and people just pop up, so to speak, in our experience. And that too is the way of it. Most of it is quite beyond our control. One day raining, the next day sunshine. What do we have to do with it? One day people come and the next day they go away. Always changing it seems, people and things. Always changing. There might be a lot of explanations as to why it's like this, but whatever the explanation, the reality is that life just seems to move along all by itself and things happen. The reality is that you're here now, a part of it, a part of this changing landscape. For whatever reason. In this particular body, which does all kinds of fascinating things, like take you on trips, wash dishes, make love, go to work, drive cars, and which also gets sick, breaks down, grows old, and finally dies.

It's a great mystery, but mystery or not, that is the way of it.

What a life!

So what's to worry?

Why can't we just let it move along at its own pace and enjoy the ride instead of mucking it up all the time? Which is what a lot of us do, or at least it's what I often do.

How do we muck it up? Mainly we muck it up by fighting the way of it.

In short, we muck it up by resisting what is.

We muck it up by telling ourselves stories about how things should be when the reality is that things just aren't the way we think they should be. Period. Full stop.

Resisting is stressful

So what does this have to do with happiness?

A lot. Because it's very stressful to resist what is. It's very stressful and tiring to fight reality all the time. And that's precisely what we're doing when we think that things should be different from what they are. We're resisting this moment. We're saying no to what is. We're basically saying the sun should be shining when it's raining. And you know how much that helps. What can you do about the rain? The only thing thinking it should be sunny when it's raining does is make you feel frustrated and unhappy. Better to deal with it and buy an umbrella! This is not difficult to see when it comes to the weather. But what about when it comes to all the other areas of our lives like our relationships, for example, or our bodies? What happens when something breaks down and you think it shouldn't? What happens then? You resist what is. And how does that make you feel?

An experiment

Let's try a little experiment.

Just think how you would feel if you didn't resist what is, just for a few minutes. And I'm not joking when I make this suggestion. In fact it's a very interesting experiment. So let's try it and see how would it feel if we didn't resist what is, if we simply couldn't resist the way things are. If we could just for a moment allow things to be exactly the way they are, without fighting them.

If you play around with this idea or mind shift, you will discover that it can be quite liberating.

So please give it a try.

You can start by putting this book down and letting yourself feel this thought, this shift in perspective, for the next couple of minutes. Just say to yourself, "For the next couple of minutes, I'm not going to fight what is. I'm just going to totally let whatever is happening, be. Whatever it is, I'm just going to accept it." If for example you have a headache or you're not feeling well, you could say to yourself, "I'm not going to fight the fact that I have a headache and am feeling lousy. I'm not going to resist my headache or what my body is doing at the moment. I'm not going to resist the discomfort I'm feeling and think that there is something wrong with me because I don't feel as good as I think I should feel. Nor am I going to tell myself a story about what this feeling of discomfort might mean. I'm not going to imagine that I'm coming down with the flu or have a brain tumor. No I'm just going to let it be and accept what's going on right now. Without having any opinion about it at all." Please give it a try right now.

When you do this for a couple of minutes, you will probably experience a huge sense of relief almost immediately. No matter how lousy you may be feeling, the moment you accept what is, you will feel everything in you relaxing and falling into place. You will feel peaceful. It's quite amazing what happens when you shift your focus.

Why? Because the way it is, is the way it is. And this is what is at this very moment. And when you accept what is, you find strangely enough, that all there is left is a feeling of peace, and then you feel happy despite your troubles!

Only a thought in your mind

So we discover that all our experiences are just thoughts in our minds. When we resist what is by telling ourselves that things shouldn't be the way they are, we make ourselves feel bad. That's really all there is to it. Events both inner and outer are just that – they are events. But it is our interpretations of these inner and outer events that make us feel good or bad, happy or sad.

Most of us are unaware that we are doing this when things happen. We don't realize that something happens and then we immediately click into our interpretations of events or our stories, which are often dire predictions based on past conditioning and beliefs about life that we've never questioned. And that's where the fight with reality begins – and all the anguish that goes with it.

Either we scare ourselves to death or we drive ourselves crazy with all our 'shoulds'. 'I should be feeling better.' 'I should have more energy.' 'I should be able to do this.' We're very good at beating ourselves up with all our 'shoulds'. But reality is what it is and the rest is all just thoughts in our minds. And our thoughts are nothing more than our interpretation of what is happening. They are not the direct experience itself, but only our interpretation. And it's our interpretation that we are living. How often are we living an experience directly, without the filter of our thoughts and opinions?

When I understood this, I suddenly saw life and everything that is going on in a new light.

I saw how much my own resistance to what is was causing me pain and anguish. I saw how my own interpretation and stories were preventing me from experiencing life directly and from seeing events for what they are. This new awareness has helped me to begin to see things more directly, without my old stories.

Nothing external...

That was when I understood that external events and things cannot disturb us. This may be a very difficult concept to understand and accept when we first hear it, but it is true nevertheless. Nothing external can disturb us because the truth is we are only experiencing our own thoughts and stories – and almost never the reality that is before us. We think and tell ourselves stories about what events, people, and things mean and then we get to live our stories. This is our only experience.

We tell ourselves that this event means this or that and that this is something bad, dangerous, or life threatening and then we experience it. But the event is just the event – with no opinion or intrinsic value one way or the other. And this holds true for all events, including death.

If this is the first time you've met this concept, you will probably find it shocking and extremely challenging. I know because I still find it shocking and extremely challenging even though I've been contemplating this for quite a while now. It's difficult to understand and accept because it's such a radical shift in perspective from everything we've learned and were taught to believe about life. But that doesn't make it any less true.

And if it is true, the consequences are very far-reaching and, fortunately for us, very liberating.

If it is true, and my experience demonstrates for me that it is, it means for example that if you or I have a serious illness like cancer or multiple sclerosis or any other so-called 'serious' problem or handicap we can be just as happy as someone who doesn't have these so-called problems. Because it is only our interpretation of what is happening that can make us unhappy. Only the story we are telling ourselves about what our situations mean can make us unhappy. Because the truth is that at this very moment, no matter what our problem, we are still breathing, we're still here, and life still is. Our unhappiness arises the minute we compare ourselves to other people or to what we think we should be doing and feeling at this particular moment. But if we stop comparing, what's left?

If we drop our thoughts about the meaning of what's going on, what do we have? And I'm not talking about right or wrong here, but just about what is actually going on.

The first thing I always notice – when I let go of my thoughts about the meaning of what's going on – is that suddenly it gets very peaceful. The second thing I notice is there's only me here now. And that's about it. This moment with whatever is. The sun on my face for example. Or this moment, doing the dishes. This moment, gazing at the flowers in the vase next to me. Or this moment, sitting in front of my computer.

That's about it.

Plain and simple.

Life.

Peace.

Happiness.

The truth is you and I can lead happy lives regardless of our situation. Because when we drop our interpretation of events, we find that happiness is our nature. Our natural state. It's what we are. We may have been brought up to think otherwise, to think that our happiness depends on our health, on outside circumstances, on our good looks, or on the amount of money we have in the bank, but it's just not true.

We can live happy lives regardless because happiness is our

innermost nature. It has nothing to do with health, money or success. In fact, it has nothing to do with anything outside of us because we can only experience our own thoughts, which means nothing external can influence our happiness one way or the other unless we allow it to. Only our interpretations of what's going on can influence our experience. That in fact is what your life is. Your life is your interpretation of what's going on. My life (or we could say my experience) is my interpretation of what's going on. And that means we have nothing to deal with but our own thoughts – and that nothing but our own thoughts can prevent us from living a happy life right this very moment.

It's a mind-boggling discovery isn't it? That we have nothing to deal with but our own thoughts? And even though I have been saying this for years in all my books, the ramifications of this discovery just keep expanding for me as my understanding of this simple statement – *we have nothing to deal with but our own thoughts* – continues to grow.

> **Unhappiness is only a thought in your mind.**

Once I got over the shock of discovering that unhappiness was just a thought in my mind, I realized that without the thought, without my interpretation of events, where was the unhappiness?

What about pain?

So I tried to take this discovery one step further. To the worst we can imagine, like pain. And I asked myself what is pain? And I realized that pain too must be a thought because without the thought of pain, where's the pain? For example, if we're in pain and we fall asleep, what happens to the pain? Think about it. If you have a headache and you fall asleep, where's the pain? Where does it go while you are sleeping and not thinking about the headache? And then you wake up and the headache is back. Or what about when you're at work and have a headache and then you get so involved in what you're doing that you forget the headache for a while, but as soon as you think about it, it's back. So the question is what happens to the pain when we don't think about it? Which again made me see that without thought, what is there? Where's the pain without the thought?

So I tried to experiment with pain too to see what happens. Instead of just going to sleep, I tried consciously changing my focus when I was in pain. And I found that the pain didn't disappear when I consciously changed my focus but that the quality of the pain did change. And I discovered something else: I found that when I think about a pain, I am mostly resisting the pain and that when I resist pain it definitely gets worse. Now what do I mean by resisting pain? By resisting pain I mean telling myself a story about the pain and what it might mean. For example, if I'm in pain and I get in a panic and think things like, "Oh this is awful. What's wrong with me? Is my condition dangerous? Will it last a long time? What if it gets worse! What will happen if it gets worse? Could it be something serious like cancer? If it's something serious I might die!" Or one of the many other scary thoughts we think when we are in pain. I found when I do this the pain definitely seems to intensify and get worse.

This discovery made me wonder how much of the suffering we associate with pain has to do with the physical pain itself and how much it has to do with the stories we are telling ourselves when we are in pain. So now when I experience pain, I try to be with myself without telling myself a story about what the pain could mean for my life and my future. I try to be with the sensation in the present moment and allow it, without going into a panic. When I am able to do this, I find the nature of the discomfort changes. The pain doesn't go away, but the intensity lessens.

If this rings a bell for you, I suggest you give it a try the next time you experience pain. See if you can just be with your discomfort in the present moment. Take your medicine and take whatever other practical steps are necessary to deal with the situation, but see if you can drop the story you are telling yourself about the consequences of the pain you are experiencing. Just forget all about it. Don't project anything into the future, but stay in the present moment. Because the truth is that you are in the present and you cannot know for sure what the pain means or what is going to happen. All you can know for sure is that you are here now and that there is discomfort. And then see what happens.

What a sage says

In my studies, I found this interesting analysis of the difference between pain and suffering in a talk by the famous Indian sage Sri Nisargadatta Maharaj,

"Pain is physical, suffering is mental. Beyond the mind there is no suffering. Pain is merely a signal that the body is in danger and requires attention... Pain is essential for the survival of the body, but none compels you to suffer. Suffering is due entirely to clinging or resisting; it is a sign of our unwillingness to move on, to flow with life."

From the book, *I Am That – Talks with Sri Nisargadatta Maharaj.*

Concepts don't help

Since this is a book about happiness, we're not looking at our concepts of right or wrong but simply at what makes us happy or unhappy. So it's not a question of whether or not you should be in pain, nor is it a question of whether it's fair that you are in pain. We're not talking about fair; we're talking about reality. We're talking about what is. And if you are feeling pain, well then that's your reality – whether or not it's fair. And if being in pain is your present reality, what is the best way to deal with this situation? It's definitely not by scaring yourself to death or by telling yourself it's not fair and that you don't deserve to feel this way. What good is a story like that going to do for you? How is a story like that going to improve the quality of your life when you are in pain? What is your day going to be like when you tell yourself things like this?

The truth of the matter is that if we want to be happy with the way our lives really are at this moment, we will probably have to question and go beyond some of our most cherished beliefs and concepts. Because what good are these beliefs and concepts doing if they are making us unhappy? What can we use them for?

The little girl in Afghanistan

When we discuss this, one of my friends always asks me, "What about the little girl in Afghanistan who got her leg blown off by a landmine?" Well what about the little girl in Afghanistan? Does our story about how unfair life is improve the quality of her life in any way? And I'm not saying we shouldn't do everything we can to ease suffering and make this world a better place. I'm just saying that her reality right now is one leg. That's reality. Nothing we can do can change that or bring her leg back. And who's to say if we aren't just projecting our own fears and stories about how we think life should be on this little girl? We can't know for sure what she is thinking and experiencing. But let's say it's true that she is telling herself the same story that we're telling ourselves about how unfairly life has treated her. How will that story help her live her life when her reality is one leg? Nothing is going to change the reality of her one leg. So what are we saying? Are we saying that because she only has one leg, she has less life than you or I? Does it mean she's condemned to eternal unhappiness because she's only got one leg? Is her life an utter waste because she's only got one leg or what? Is there no joy for her because she's lost her leg? Because if that's the story we're telling (or she's telling), that's even crueler than the loss of her leg!

The reality is, with or without her leg, she is here and there is life.

The reality is, with or without her leg, she has as much life as anyone else.

The reality is, with or without her leg, she has the great gift of consciousness.

I think part of our resistance to reality in situations like this with the little girl in Afghanistan stems from our cherished belief that a whole body and material comfort are prerequisites and fundamental requirements for living a happy life. That seems to be one of our most cherished beliefs here in the West. And again I am not saying we shouldn't work for social justice and to ease suffering and improve life for everyone on earth. That is not what I'm saying. What I'm saying is we need to question this concept – that a whole body and material comfort are necessary for our happiness. We need to ask ourselves if we can really and truly know that this is true. If happiness is our nature, can we know for sure that without a whole body and the material comforts of life, we are doomed to unhappiness? Can we know for sure that if we are missing a leg and don't have running water, a fancy kitchen, and a refrigerator filled with food that we are doomed to unhappiness? Because if that is true, then we are saying that the poverty-stricken little girl in Afghanistan with one leg blown off is, now and forever, cut off from life and happiness! And how can we know that that's true?

Nothing passive about it

But you ask, does accepting what is, mean becoming passive in the face of life? Does accepting what is, mean just saying 'yes' to everything and not dealing with suffering or doing what's needed to make yourself or other people feel better? Does it mean you can't act or work to improve conditions and life on earth?

At first glance, many people might feel that accepting what is seems to mean passivity, but in reality it means just the opposite. Why? Because when you see what's really going on clearly and calmly, when you are able to see what is happening at this moment, without being hysterical or resisting what already is, you are in a much better position to deal with the situation in the best possible way.

If you are walking down the street and someone has a heart attack right in front of you, that is what is. You can't change that by yelling and screaming and being hysterical won't do the person much good nor will thinking 'Poor man, this shouldn't have happened. He doesn't deserve this.' But being fully present and calmly calling an ambulance will help him. And so will loosening his clothes, making him comfortable, holding his hand, and doing whatever your heart and wisdom tells you to do.

And this is true for all the other big and little things and events we resist in our daily lives. Instead of wasting so much of our energy resisting what is, we can choose to be present and deal as kindly and as wisely as we can with what is happening.

> **Whatever is happening is what should be happening.**
> **Why? Because it is happening.**

When we start working with these ideas and watch and observe our minds and our thoughts, we discover that without our stories and concepts about what 'should' or 'shouldn't' be happening in our lives at this moment, our true nature is revealed to us. And we find happiness right here in the present moment in all its mystery, wonder and glory.

> **Happiness is our nature.**

Which leads to the next point...

No. 2

Want what you have

The number 2 cause of suffering and unhappiness is wanting what you don't have.

Are you suffering from what I call the 'never good enough' syndrome? Are you always wanting more than what is? And are you beating yourself up because you don't have it? Are you convinced that what you had before was better than what you have now? And that what you have now is not as good as what your neighbors have or what your best friend has. Are you also quite sure that your health isn't as good as it used to be and that the weather isn't either. Do you have a sneaking suspicion that the weather was better in the good old days? And that the state of the economy was too? Or at least the state of your economy was? And when it comes to your clothes, do you feel that they're not as good as your friends' clothes nor is your sofa come to think of it. Not to mention your TV which isn't the latest model with the latest hi-tech finesses either. Also do you feel that it's unfair that your rent is higher than it used to be and that the cost of living just keeps going up just like the prices in the supermarket?

Or maybe you feel that life was more exciting when you were younger or that life will be more exciting when you get older? Or that life will be more satisfying when you graduate from university and get a good job or when you get married and have a family. Or maybe you're convinced that if you had a boyfriend/girlfriend you could count on everything would be so much better and you'd finally be safe. Does any of this sound like you? If it does, then you're suffering from what I call the 'never good enough' syndrome!

No wonder you're not happy!

Think about what's going on in your mind! It's a war zone! It's a constant battle with reality. No wonder you feel stressed and unhappy.

If this is anything like you, maybe it's time you ask yourself what good all these constant comparisons are doing you? How do they and your stories and expectations improve the quality of your life here and now? The reality is your rent and the cost of living are going up. The reality is your health isn't as good as it used to be and your TV isn't the latest model and your sofa is worn out. The reality is you don't have a wife and kids and the perfect family. So let's face it, according to the stories you're telling yourself, you're never going to be OK or happy. And it's all because of the stories you're telling yourself about how your life should be, when the reality is your life isn't like that.

If this isn't insanity, what is?

Who sets the standards?

Let's take a closer look at some examples of this kind of story for a moment. Because we're all telling stories all the time, including me.

When I started examining the stories I was telling myself about how my life should be, it was quite a shock. And I felt the same sense of shock and surprise when I really started listening to the stories I heard other people telling me (and themselves) about their lives. (When you start examining our stories – whether they are your own or other people's – you will discover that most of our stories are pretty similar. We are all doing variations on the same themes!)

Anyway, I realized that all these stories we are telling ourselves and each other are based on totally arbitrary standards and rules about how life should be. Here are some examples of what they might sound like: When I graduate from university and get a high-powered job, I'll be a success (and be happy). When I achieve prominence in my field, I'll be a success (and be happy). When I make a lot of money, I'll be a success (and be happy). When I look good and have lots of fashionable clothes, I'll be a success (and be happy). When I marry a guy with a good job, have a nice house and two children, I'll be a success (and be happy). When I make a great discovery in my field, I'll be a success (and be happy). When I demonstrate that I am a good manager and get a promotion, I'll be a success (and be happy). When my children get good grades in school, I'll be a success (and be happy). When my body is functioning well, I'll be a success (and be happy). According to these stories, if and when you achieve these things and are a success, you'll be happy. But is that true?

Let's look again. And try to find out if it really works like this or not.

Let's take three scenarios and examine them.

Situation 1): A job at McDonald's.
You're unemployed and really broke. You get a job at McDonald's and think it's just great. You feel like a success.

You were the managing director of a big company and just got fired. A friend says oh well you can always get a job at McDonalds. To you a job at McDonald's would be the ultimate humiliation and defeat.

Situation 2): Walking with crutches.
You have multiple sclerosis and are stuck in a wheelchair most of the time. Now with the help of your physical therapist, you are learning to hobble around on crutches. It's a great success for you.

You're a really active person and just broke your foot while you were out running. Now you have to hobble around on crutches for the next 2 months. This doesn't feel very successful.

Situation 3): You get pregnant.
You've been trying to get pregnant for several years now and have been getting all kinds of fertility treatments. Now finally you're pregnant. You're overjoyed. Getting pregnant is the success you've been dreaming about.

You already have three kids and the last thing you need is another mouth to feed. Getting pregnant is not your idea of success.

These are just three examples of the same situation. Are they successes or failures? Do they make you happy or unhappy? The situations are just what they are. The determining factor is the way you react in each situation. In other words, it is the story you are telling about the meaning of these events that determines if the situations make you happy or unhappy. In themselves, the events have no significance, no meaning. They are just things that happen. Our reaction to an external event is always an internal event.

So who is the judge of your success or failure? Who or what has the power to make you happy or unhappy? Have you looked at the way you react to external events? Have you examined the stories you are telling yourself about what these events mean?

Internal cause and effect
If you want to know the truth, there is only one place to look and that's inside yourself. This is because *all cause and effect is an internal event.* You will discover this is true when you examine your relationship to the things that happen in your life and discover that your reaction to any situation or event is based on the stories you are telling yourself about life and the meaning of these situations and events. Your reaction is determined by your expectations, which are determined by your definition of what is good or bad. And these value judgments are based on so many things – for example on your background, your culture, your

religion, your sex, your age, your country, your job, your family, and so forth.

So your reaction to anything that happens is totally arbitrary and has nothing to do with anything – except your own value judgments.

This means that when something happens, if we think it's good, we feel happy. If we think it's bad, we feel unhappy. It's as simple as that. But regardless of our reaction, the event is still the event. In truth, there is no connection whatsoever between an event and your reaction to it. The way you experience the event has absolutely nothing to do with the event itself.

Things just happen

When we start to see this, we realize that things just happen and then we judge them and react to them based on our stories about what we believe is good or bad and on our ideas of how reality should be in order to live up to our idea of what's good. That's the mechanism and if you are happy with your life, well that's just fine. But if you're not happy, you might want to ask yourself what your standards for happiness and success are and who is setting these standards for you? Did you really and truly set these standards for yourself or have your just accepted the belief systems of your family, friends, peers, school, workplace, culture and society? And if this is what you are doing, what kind of stories are you telling yourself about the way things 'should' be? Are you aware of your stories? Have you thought about the belief systems your stories are based on?

If you aren't completely happy with your life, if you spend a lot of time wanting what you don't have, it might be a good idea to take a closer look at your expectations. When you do this, you might discover that you are setting yourself up for failure and unhappiness without being aware of what you're doing.

Unfortunately until we wake up, most of us are not setting our own standards. Rather we are unconscious and go through life judging our experiences according to standards and beliefs we are not even aware of. There is nothing new or unusual about this. We are all doing this. Until we become aware of it, most of us just blindly accept the ideas, standards and expectations that are propagated in the societies we live in. These messages and belief systems are all around us and we are constantly getting cues from our families and friends, from the media and television, from our schools and workplaces, from our politicians and leaders. And we blindly accept many of these beliefs, standards and stories because that's the way we are brought up. No one has taught us to question these beliefs. No one has taught us to ask ourselves – is it true? Is this good for me? Will it make me happy? No one has taught us to really 'see' what's going on. And no one has taught us to see the difference between reality and our stories.

So for many of us, it's not until we find ourselves deeply unhappy or in crisis that we start to question our beliefs and begin to wake up. There's nothing like a good crisis to force one to take the time to investigate and question what we really believe. When we do this, there's a very good chance that we may well discover the connection between our stories, our standards, our value judgments – and our happiness and well being.

**Everything is a success
if you don't have any expectations.**

The blessing of crisis

When the beauty of inner work starts to unfold for us, we discover the true meaning of our crises! What would we do without our crises? Who would we be if we never met a good crisis? Just think about it. Without our crises, most of us would never grow or develop! We'd just stay stuck in our ruts and continue to be distracted by all the trivialities around us. But fortunately, most of us are blessed with crisis – that wonderful magic wand of change – that either nudges us gently or kicks us in the butt, forcing us to ask questions and perhaps even wake up!

Crisis is an alarm signal, a sign that something you are thinking or doing is preventing you from experiencing the happiness that is your true nature and birthright.

There's another interesting thing about crisis. When we are young and inexperienced, we have a tendency to be terrified when we find ourselves in crisis especially if we have not been taught the value of crisis or how to investigate our thinking. Then as life goes on and we survive one or several major crises, we mature and begin to understand that we can probably deal with crisis and may even survive! We may even discover that what we once thought of as a crisis is really nothing more than our own inappropriate reaction to events that are quite beyond our control!

I remember I once read a study about the men who survived German submarines that were sunk during the war. To the researchers' great surprise, they found that when the survivors were rescued after many days lost at sea, it was mostly the older men who survived the ordeal while many of the younger men perished (even though they were stronger and more fit than the older men). It seems that when the men had to abandon their ships and struggle to survive in lifeboats on the open sea, the young men were more terrified than the older ones who had lived longer and seen and survived crisis before. In this case as in so many others, survival can be a question of attitude.

Another way of defining crisis could be: Resisting what is!

So instead of running from what we call 'a crisis' and our anxious feelings, we eventually learn to stand quietly and take a good look at what's going on. When we shine the light of awareness on events (also those we call a crisis) and our reactions to these events, amazing things happen.

> **What is crisis? Resisting what is.**

Who would you be?

So whether you consider yourself to be in crisis or not, sooner or later we discover that it's all a question of dealing with our own thoughts and reactions to events and circumstances. When we realize this, it becomes obvious to ask – who would I be without my arbitrary standards and stories about what it takes to be happy?

Let's take a look. Without your stories, what's left?

This makes everything very concrete.

What do you actually have right now?

What is your reality right now?

The first thing you notice is you are here now, inhabiting this body or so it seems. However you want to explain it to yourself, the reality is *you are here now.* Period. Full stop. That's it. That's reality. That is what is. You exist and you are here now. You have this life. Nothing could be more obvious than this, but we have a tendency to overlook this most basic (and amazing) fact – the wonder of our own existence. And why do we forget? Because we're all so caught up in our stories, we're all so distracted, that we miss what is. We miss *being here now.* We miss *life.* We miss it even though it's happening right in front of our eyes. Instead we're so lost in our heads that we fail to see what's right in front of us and overlook the most basic and precious thing we have – our very own existence. It's really quite amazing when you think about it. To discover that we forgot the most precious gift of all, that we are! That we're alive. That we are life itself, right here and right now.

But when you get it, when it registers, you suddenly see the wonder of what is right in front of you. The present moment in all its glory. And that's all there is.

Success and happiness

So let's go back to the beginning and ask ourselves: Is there really any link at all between success and happiness? Now that we've discovered that success is just a story about something external that we think we need in order to be happy, what do concepts like these have to do with true happiness? If nothing external can affect us and it's all a question of internal cause and effect, how can anything external make us a success or make us happy?

So what makes us happy?

Here's what I've discovered – happiness is a mind that is at peace with itself. A mind that is fully present and that is not resisting what is. A mind that is not telling stories about how things 'should' be when they are not. A mind that is at peace with the way things are and the way people are. A mind that is not at war with the present situation, but that is awake and alert and can deal with what is happening in this now moment. What other success can there be? What other pathway to happiness?

> **Ultimately success is to be happy with your thoughts. Because what else is there?**

A new strategy

So why not try a new strategy? Since we all know that we suffer when we want what we don't have, why not try a new strategy and decide to want what you have instead? Is that such a weird idea? Well just think about it for a moment. It's really very simple. We just found out that our unhappiness arises from wanting what we don't have. So why not want what you have instead!

Let's take a closer look at this mechanism.

Take a moment and bring yourself home to yourself. Now ask yourself – and answer as honestly as you can – what is making you unhappy right now, right this very moment? Chances are it's because you don't have what you want – or because you have what you don't want, which is just another way of saying the same thing. Is this true or not? Be honest with yourself. The only thing that can be preventing you from being happy right now is wanting something you don't have. Maybe it's better health, maybe it's more sunshine, maybe it's a nicer apartment, maybe it's a partner who's more understanding, maybe it's more money in the bank, but whatever it is, it's something you don't have at this very moment in time. And this is what's making you unhappy now. Is what I am saying true or not? What else could be making you unhappy at this very moment? It can only be the thought of what you don't have that's making you miserable. So why not decide to want what you have and be happy instead? This is not as crazy as it sounds, especially when you realize that all our experiences are just thoughts in our mind anyway. There's no escaping this fact – *every single experience we are having is just a thought in our mind* – every single one of them. There is nothing else going on. Even though some of these thoughts (and experiences) are thoughts and experiences we like and therefore desire while others are thoughts (and experiences) we dislike and therefore resist. However you look at it, that's all that's going on. Thoughts in your mind, which you either like or dislike. And that's about it. The situations in themselves, the specific events and circumstances that we like or dislike, really don't have much to do with it at all. They are just the happenings of being alive that are unfolding before us. It's our preferences that make us happy or sad.

> **Why not want what you have
> instead of wanting what you don't have?
> This is the fast route to a happy life.**

Experiment with wanting what you have

So let's experiment for a moment with wanting what we have. First of all put down this book and take a good look at what you have at this very moment in your life. Look at what you're doing, look at where you're sitting, become aware of what and how you're feeling, and notice what's going on around you. Take it all in – whatever it is. Don't be judgmental in any way, just look around and see what's going on around you in your life right now. Both externally and internally. Then take a deep breath and ask yourself how you would feel if you really and truly wanted exactly and precisely all of this right now. How would it feel if you could only want this? If you could only want everything that is happening around you right now as well as everything that's going on inside you? How would it feel if you really felt this? If you really felt that whatever it is – was absolutely perfect for you? If you really felt that you didn't want to change anything at all? Take a leap in your imagination and try and see what happens!

How does it feel?

Give yourself a chance to really feel what it feels like to want precisely what you have at this moment.

And then let it sink in.

It feels like instant peace, doesn't it!

No. 3

Be honest with yourself

> **The number 3 cause of suffering and unhappiness is not communicating honestly with yourself.**

Do you realize you are the one person you're going to spend the rest of your life with? Do you understand that you are the closest person to you? And that you will always be the closest person to you? The one person in the whole world who will never ever leave you. No matter what. Do you realize that no one, no matter what they do nor how hard they try, is ever going to get closer to you than you? And even if you know this, have you taken the time to really get close to yourself so that you truly and honestly know who you are? My guess is probably not. Why do I say this? Because strangely enough, so few people seem to be comfortable with the idea of getting close to themselves.

Why is it like this? Why are we so afraid of looking within? Why is it so difficult for us to truly face ourselves and find out what really feels right to us? Without having to justify how we feel to anyone else? Why is it so hard to admit to ourselves the truth about ourselves? It's almost like it's taboo or something. Why do we have such difficulty knowing for ourselves in our own hearts and minds who we really are and what we really like?

Looking within

If you don't know who you are, how can you live a happy life? And if you say your life is happy right now, I might ask – a happy life for whom? How can you know who is living your happy life if you don't know who you are? Some people are living happy lives for their husbands. Some for their wives. Some for their children. Others are living happy lives for their parents. What about you? Whose happy life are you living? Is it your own or someone else's? Because the question is how can you honor yourself and make good choices for yourself if you don't even know who you are? How can you do it if you haven't taken the time to sit down with yourself and find out what's right for you? And if you don't know what makes you tick, how can you take proper care of you?

You can only take care of yourself if you know yourself.

You can only make good choices for yourself if you know yourself.

You can only set limits if you know yourself.

But to know yourself you have to be able to answer basic questions like:

- What do you really like (not what you think you 'should' like or what other people think you 'should' like)
- What's OK for you
- What's not OK for you
- What makes you feel good
- What makes you feel uncomfortable
- What you find unacceptable
- Where your limits are

You can only find the answers to these questions by going inside and asking yourself humbly and honestly. Can you sit quietly with yourself and find out? And answer just for you. Again not for someone else – not for your wife, your husband, your boyfriend, your kids, your parents, or your friends?

The way you are

If you really want to answer these questions, you must realize that to answer honestly you don't have to explain to anyone why you are the way you are. You are you and you are the way you

28

are, for whatever reasons. You don't have to justify yourself to anyone. It's as simple as that. You have the right to be you, whatever that means, but you must accept the consequences of being you. By this I mean there is no right and wrong way to be you, but in this universe where we live, there is the law of cause and effect, which is always working. And that means that whoever you are, every action has consequences. But you always have the right to think and do what you feel and believe what is best for you – and accept the consequences. Always. Because no one escapes the law of cause and effect. That's just the way it is. Which means sooner or later, you will always get to see, feel, taste, touch and live the consequences of your choices. Always. And this is exactly how it should be because how else could you learn? How else could you really discover who you are except by experiencing the effects of your choices?

Becoming your own best friend

One of the secrets of living a happy life is to become your own best friend. But you can only do this when you know who you are, when you honestly and truly know yourself. Because what does a best friend do? A best friend sees you for who you really are and unconditionally loves and supports the real you. But how can you do this for yourself if you don't honestly know who you are?

So being your own best friend means communicating honestly with yourself. And knowing who you are and not pretending to yourself (or anyone else) to be what you're not. Being your own best friend means loving yourself and taking care of yourself. It means being able to take stock of yourself and recognize your strengths and your weaknesses. It means respecting yourself for who you are and asking yourself honestly what is right for you in each situation. It means being able to set limits as to what you are willing to do for others. It means being able to ask "What can I offer in this situation that is honestly congruent with who I am and with my skills, strengths and energy level right now? So that I respect and honor myself, while respecting and honoring the situation and the other people involved as best I can?" And then sticking to that. In other words, it means asking yourself what is appropriate in each now moment so that you can maintain your integrity, feel good about yourself, and function optimally, both today and tomorrow. For many this is a tall order, especially if you are a "people pleaser". But the truth is that to be your own best friend, you have to be able to say "no" to others without feeling guilty and without feeling that you have to explain or justify your choices or your behavior.

It's your decision

You are doing what you are doing because that's your decision. Period. No one has the right to question your right to decide for yourself (unless of course you are interfering with another person's freedom to decide for themselves). Only you can really know what's best for you, and there is no universal law that requires you to explain why. Even if well meaning people may try to convince you otherwise. And also because even if you tried to explain yourself, you probably don't honestly know why you are making the choices you are making right now anyway. You might have some superficial answers, but in truth do you know why you are like you are? Do you know why you prefer coffee for breakfast instead of tea? Or why you like to sleep on your stomach instead of on your back? Or why you prefer the evenings to the mornings? Or why you'd rather go to the mountains than lie on the beach? Or why you're an early riser even though your mate prefers to sleep late? I mean who can explain these things really? Who can explain anything when you come right down to it? And that goes for all of us. At the end of the day, there are no easy answers as to why we are the way we are, it's just the way things are. So much of our pain and anguish comes from resisting and fighting the way we are.

So find out what makes you tick and honor it!
Find out what drives you crazy and deal with it!
Find out what makes your heart sing and go for it!

Communicating honestly with yourself

It blew me away when I realized I was having so much difficulty communicating with others because I wasn't communicating honestly with myself. How could I expect to communicate clearly with others if I wasn't able to look within and honestly find out what was OK for me and what wasn't. It blew the lid off my head to realize this. And a completely new perspective on my problems came to light, which eventually helped me start learning to communicate more honestly, first with myself and then with others.

Here are some of the things I discovered along the way. First of all I realized that I was such a people pleaser and that I was so afraid of conflict. And I realized that these two modes of behavior made it very hard for me to look within and be honest with myself. It was dangerous to truly know and acknowledge what I was really feeling about things because oh my God what if the way I was and the things I wanted led to conflict? What if I wasn't acceptable? What if the way I was didn't please people? What if it upset them? What if they disapproved? What if the things I wanted were wrong? What if...? When I started to explore these issues, I found it boils down to being unclear/confused about things like:

- Being a 'people pleaser'
  - Seeking the love and approval of others
  - Believing you are being loving and kind by doing what other people want you to do
- Being afraid of disagreement/conflict
  - Believing that people 'should' agree when they don't (fighting reality)

- Believing conflict is bad, dangerous (not understanding the difference between being assertive and being aggressive)
- Having a lot of arbitrary 'shoulds'
  - Having uninvestigated codes of behavior
  - Letting other people manipulate you with their uninvestigated codes of behavior

Let's take a closer look at these common problems.

Being a people pleaser

If you're a people pleaser like I was, you are always trying to make other people happy – at all costs. And you're terrified of offending anyone with your words and/or actions. This can make life a nightmare because you are desperately seeking the love and approval of others even if it means sacrificing your own integrity and needs, or doing things you don't want to do. Seeking the approval of others is definitely the royal road to unhappiness. Why? Because no matter how hard you try and no matter what you do, someone is always going to disapprove. That's just the way it is. The reality of life is that people don't approve of each other most of the time so the chances are that no matter what you do, someone's not going to approve of you and what you are doing!

So where does that leave you and all your good intentions? Nowhere! The only thing you get out of trying to please other people is the stress of squeezing yourself out of shape in your attempt to be what you think other people want you to be. By trying to please others in this way, you end up denying yourself and making yourself anxious and miserable. And in the long run, it's a surefire way to make yourself sick and unhappy. Trying to please other people is probably one of the most stressful occupations on the planet because you are fighting a losing battle!

> **Seeking the approval of others is definitely
> the royal road to unhappiness.**

Being loving and kind

Oh but you say, you want to be loving and kind. Well what does that mean? Does being loving and kind mean being a doormat? Does being loving and kind mean choosing to please others instead of doing what you think is right and taking care of yourself? Does being loving and kind mean sacrificing your own integrity and agreeing with things or people when you know it's wrong or when it doesn't feel right to you? Does it mean being afraid to ask for the time to consider things when you're not sure of what you feel? Does it mean you can't follow your own intuition just because someone else says something different?

Being loving and kind is one of those wonderful stories we tell ourselves to confuse ourselves and to block honest communications with ourselves and with others. And who's to say if being clear and honest and communicating openly is not the most loving and kind thing we can possibly do in every situation!

Being afraid of disagreement

Another great barrier to clear and honest communication is the belief that people 'should' agree with each other. The thought that people 'should' agree with each other might be a nice idea, but in the real world, people just don't agree with each other. And they never have. Once again, we're not talking about right or wrong, we're just talking about the way things are. We're talking about reality. And as we know, when we argue with reality, we end up making ourselves miserable. So when it comes to disagreeing, the reality is that people do disagree with each other. People have different ideas and opinions about almost everything. People have different preferences about how to do things. And they have different goals, dreams, hopes, wishes, likes and dislikes. That's just the way it is. Different things interest different people. Some people love snowstorms while others love the heat. Some people think the ultimate joy is traveling to a crowded city for a busy weekend of shopping and dining out while others think the ultimate joy is retreating to a quiet spot in nature or going to a meditation center. That's just the way of it. Wanting people to agree is setting yourself up for heartache and failure because it's never going to happen.

So why are we so afraid of disagreement? Why do we want the impossible? Usually it's because we want people to like, love and approve of us. I think part of the fear of disagreement can be found in the fact that we link agreement and approval with people liking or loving us. We think that if we love someone we 'should' agree with him or her. And we think that if he/she really loves us, they 'should' agree with us. But is that true? Think of all the people you really do love. How many of them do you agree with and how many of them agree with you? Of course if your definition of love is "you agree with me and I agree with you" well then you're really in for trouble!

Agreement and love are two different things

So here's what I found out. If you want to live a happy life, it's a good idea to stop mixing up agreeing with people and love. They are two different things. If you want to save yourself a lot of hassle, wake up and separate these two things in your mind. And stop telling yourself the story that people who love each other 'should' agree with each other. Again because loving someone and agreeing with someone are two different things. So if you want to save yourself a lot of heartache, stop telling yourself that if you disagree with someone it means you don't love them – because that's probably not true. And vice versa, stop telling yourself that if they disagree with you, it means they don't love you – because that's probably not true either! Whatever the reality is (whether they love you or they don't), linking agreement and love together causes us a lot of stress. And it also makes it very difficult for us to communicate honestly with ourselves and with the people in our lives. Obviously, because if you express yourself honestly and someone disagrees, and you believe that love is based on agreeing with people, you will immediately feel that the slightest disagreement means the end of love! What a nightmare!

Is disagreement dangerous?

There's another aspect to disagreement too. Do you believe that just because people disagree, it will lead to conflict and violence? We can also be afraid of disagreement because we believe that disagreement is dangerous. We can fear that it can lead to conflict and physical violence. Is this true? Sometimes the answer to this may in fact be yes. In certain situations, disagreeing could be dangerous to your life but usually it isn't. So it is important to be able to judge the situation you're in accurately so you are able to take care of yourself in situations that could turn violent. No one expects you to disagree with someone who is violent or with someone who is pointing a gun at your head and asking for your money. When you're in situations like this, the wise thing to do is agree as fast as you can!

When I talk about the fear of disagreement, I'm not talking about extreme situations where common sense tells us to keep our mouths shut! No, I'm talking about the normal everyday exchanges that go on between people who have different ideas about how things should be done. It's here that our fear of disagreement and/or conflict may be inappropriate. It's in these normal everyday exchanges that we need to ask ourselves why we're so afraid of disagreement. Is it because there is a real threat to our physical well-being or is it simply because we have the mistaken belief that people 'should' agree with each other. If you want to improve you're ability to communicate clearly and honestly, it's worth investigating.

Find out when disagreement is dangerous and when it's not. And when it's not (which is probably most of the time), make it a point to practice disagreeing kindly and firmly until you learn that disagreeing is not dangerous to your well-being!

Taking care of yourself

Being able to disagree in an appropriate manner is a necessary skill if you want to take care of yourself and live a happy life. Which brings me back to where I started. The bottom line is you have the right to want what you want and do what you do – and accept the consequences. But as I said to begin with – to really find out what you truly want, you must start by communicating honestly with yourself. And to do this, you must first peel away the layers of conditioned responses and uninvestigated, automatic beliefs that may be making it difficult for you to communicate honestly with yourself. And this can be quite a challenge, especially if you've spent your life being a 'people pleaser'.

> **You have the right to want what you want and do what you do – and accept the consequences.**

There's another interesting aspect to the idea of 'taking care of yourself' that confuses the issue for many of us. Unfortunately many of us also 'expect' other people to take care of us. It's often another one of those cherished beliefs we haven't investigated. It's just something we believe. You might, for example, expect your husband or wife or boyfriend/girlfriend to know your needs and take care of you. Or you might expect your parents to take care of you or your children to take care of you. This is a common story, something we hear all the time – the story about people who expect other people to take care of them. But it's an interesting idea when you examine it. Because first of all, how can anyone else take care of you? And secondly, why should they? Because, you say, he/she should take care of me because he/she loves me. But is this true? Is it true that other people, i.e., our loved ones, 'should' know our needs (are they telepathic?) and take care of us because they love us? Does it go with the turf, so to speak, that people who love us should automatically know our needs and take care of us? Is there some kind of universal law that says so?

It seems to me that so many of our problems arise because we have unrealistic expectations to other people (especially the people we love), expectations that are impossible to live up to. We expect them to understand us, love us, and know our needs. And not only that, we expect them to take care of us too! (It's a zoo! No wonder we have such a hard time getting along with each other!)

Now I'm not talking about Victorian England or other societies today where women, for example, are not allowed to work and the social norm says that men must financially support their wives and children. I'm talking about our modern society here in the West where both men and women have the opportunity to get an education and both sexes have the right to work.

She doesn't understand my needs

So let's look at reality. What's really going on? Many of us get disappointed or unhappy with our loved ones because even though they do love us, they just don't understand our needs and they don't take care of us the way we want to be taken care of! This is reality. This is the way things are. Not only are other people unaware of our needs, most of them didn't sign up to take care of us even if we are in a close relationship with them. This is where it gets confusing for most of us. We have some cock-amanic belief that they 'should'. Our beliefs go like this: "He should understand me. He should know what I like. He should have known that I needed this or that." "She should have been there for me. She should help me through this. She should wait for me. She should…" The list is endless. But the question is – should she? Should he? What's the reality? The reality is probably that even though this person does love you, they're often not there for you when you think they should be. And you're probably often not there for them either. (Remember it works both ways.) But no matter how we cut the cake, it comes back to ourselves.

> **Counting on other people to fix things for us because they 'should' is a surefire way to be unhappy.**

Who can you count on?

So who can we count on? We are the only ones we can count on. Once when I was having relationship problems and was in therapy, my therapist said to me, "Since you can't count on him that leaves only you!" It struck me like a bolt of lightening. It was so true. Who could I count on beside myself? Who could really know my needs and take care of them but me? It was a big break-through for me because I realized that expecting the man in my life to understand me and take care of me was a surefire way to set myself up for heartache. Because the reality was it never happened. And the reality was it would never happen either. There was no way I could get him to understand my needs and honor them, even if he did love me. And what right did I have to expect him to do so? Did I understand him and respect and honor his needs? It was like a bad MTV video – with all this undying love stuff we feed ourselves from morning to evening. And instead of looking reality in the eye and realizing that I am responsible for me and for taking care of my needs, I expected him to do my job! No wonder I was unhappy!

It made me see that you can love and honor your partner until you are blue in the face, but you can never truly know another person and their changing needs and wants. It's hard enough to figure out your own! Which brings me back to where I started...!

It's your job

It's your job to take care of you! So be honest with yourself. Figure out who you are and what's right for you. Figure out what you need. Respect yourself for being you and respect your needs too. And don't expect other people to respect you if you don't. No one else is going to give you the respect you think you deserve until you do. When you respect yourself, other people probably will too (even if they don't like you). That's just the way it is. When you know who you are and what your limits are, other people usually respect you for that. When you know what's good for you and what's not, it's also much easier to be present in this now moment and communicate clearly and honestly with the people around you. When you know what's acceptable to you and what's not, it's much easier to deal with situations as they arise because you will know where you stand and can act accordingly.

This is what happens when you communicate honestly with yourself.

This is what happens when you know and respect yourself.

It makes everything a lot easier and it's a great way to live.

Also because once you figure out who you are and get comfortable with that, it's also a lot easier to let go of the belief that you 'should' be able to explain or justify being you. When you are comfortable with you, you are more comfortable with life – and you are more willing and able to accept the fact that you really don't know why things are like they are and you probably never will.

The reality is you are you and that has consequences. You see that now because as you grow, you see that everything has consequences. That's just the way it is. So being you – whatever that means – has consequences. And that is your life story.

The reality is you are you – and that has consequences.

Learning to communicate honestly with others

Now that we've looked into communicating honestly with ourselves, what does it take to communicate honestly with other people?

First of all – as described above – it takes knowing your own mind. But when it comes to communicating honestly with others, knowing yourself isn't enough. Communicating with others is a skill – but not necessarily a skill we're born with! Of course some people are natural-born communicators, but most of us aren't. But even if you weren't born a communicator, don't despair – there's still hope. Fortunately for us, communicating honestly, openly and directly is a skill we can all learn. And in this connection, learning to be assertive is a key factor. So let's take a look at the idea of assertiveness.

Assertiveness

First of all, what does being assertive mean? Assertiveness means the ability to express yourself and defend your rights without violating the rights of others. It is appropriate, direct and open communication.

Being assertive is not the same as being aggressive. This is a very important distinction so I will repeat it. *Assertiveness is not the same as aggression.* Some people get the wrong idea and think assertiveness is aggression, but it's not. Aggression is self-enhancing behavior at the expense of others. Being assertive is just the opposite and translates into the ability to take care of oneself without violating the rights of other people.

Unfortunately, many of us confuse open and honest communication with angry and aggressive behavior – and as a result, we
are afraid of saying honestly what we feel and mean.

When I finally understood the beauty of assertiveness I
realized it was the key to taking care of myself and communicating honestly and clearly with other people at the same time. I
realized that if I could learn to be assertive, it is possible to cope
with disagreement and conflict without going to pieces. I also
found that being assertive is a firm, yet satisfying way to stand
up for your rights without becoming angry or aggressive.

In order to illustrate the difference between being assertive
and being aggressive or passive, I've developed the chart below.

Passive behavior	Assertive behavior	Aggressive behavior
Flight	**Balance Point**	**Fight**
Running away	Your own power	Attacking
Submissive	Staying in your power	Dominating
Violating your own limits	Minding your own business	Violating the limits of others
Criticizing yourself	Taking responsibility for yourself	Criticizing others
Making yourself wrong	Standing up for your rights	Making others wrong
Pointing the finger at yourself	Self-power	Pointing the finger at others

This chart shows that there is a balance point between the extremes of passive and aggressive behavior – and this balance point is assertive behavior. When you are assertive, you are staying in your own business and standing up for yourself and your rights. When you are passive, you run away from conflict and make yourself wrong. When you are aggressive, you attack and make other people wrong. The balanced position is assertive behavior – and means not going to extremes to deal with the situation but standing firm in your own power.

Your assertive rights

I first became aware of the concept of assertiveness when I read Manuel J. Smith's wonderful book *When I say no, I feel guilty* many years ago. In his book, he carefully explains the concept of assertiveness and explores many of the underlying beliefs we have that prevent us from expressing ourselves clearly and from taking care of ourselves.

In the book, he presents a list of what he calls our 10 assertive rights. I include the list for you here because it is such a revelation. For more details, please read his book. It's a true gem.

"Assertive Rights

1. You have the right to judge your own behavior, thoughts, and emotions, and to take the responsibility for their initiation and consequences upon yourself.
2. You have the right to offer no reasons or excuses to justify your behavior.
3. You have the right to judge whether you are responsible for finding solutions to other people's problems.
4. You have the right to change your mind.
5. You have the right to make mistakes – and be responsible for them.
6. You have the right to say 'I don't know'.

7. You have the right to be independent of the goodwill of others before coping with them.
8. You have the right to be illogical in making decisions.
9. You have the right to say, 'I don't understand'.
10. You have the right to say, 'I don't care'.

You have the right to say no, without feeling guilty."

From *When I say no, I feel guilty* by Manuel J. Smith

Expressing yourself assertively

So how do we express ourselves assertively when disagreement arises? What does it mean? Here are some of the main things we need to be aware of and remember when we practice expressing ourselves in an assertive manner. (And remember, learning to be assertive takes practice. You have to keep trying – again and again!)

First of all, when you disagree with someone, state your position or point of view as clearly as you can. No need to get upset. Try to be present and firm. But don't expect the other person to agree with you! Being assertive doesn't have anything to do with winning arguments or being right. Being assertive is about honestly expressing your point of view and taking care of yourself. It's not about winning and losing. So state your position clearly – and be willing to hear the other person's point of view. When you have stated your position, don't expect the other person to agree with you. He or she probably won't. When the other person has stated their position, don't be afraid to repeat your own position or point of view again, kindly but firmly. When you see or hear that the other person does not agree with you, don't attack or criticize him or her. Just stay in your own business and repeat your own position. Remember – you are responsible for your feelings and opinions about the matter. The other person is responsible for his or her feelings and opinions about the matter. Each person has a right to his/her feelings and opinions. It's also important to remember that you don't have to offer explanations or excuses for your choices, opinions, beliefs or behavior. (You might want to explain but you don't have to. Remember you have the right to be you!)

In most disagreements, the best possible outcome is what is called a 'workable compromise' – in other words a solution that both parties can accept. So it's not a question of right or wrong or of one person winning and the other losing. It's more about finding a way to deal with the matter that both people can live with if possible. (And sometimes it's just not possible. That's also reality.)

It is also important in disagreements to show the other person that you recognize them and hear what they are saying. You don't want to make the other person wrong just because he/she doesn't agree with you – and you don't want to make yourself wrong either. But you do want to acknowledge that you hear the other person's point of view and respect their feelings about the matter. This is the respectful, yet assertive way to be.

And finally, remember you don't need to agree with the other person to find a workable compromise. Once both parties understand each other's position, it can be much easier to find a solution that both parties can accept.

So to summarize, here are the main points to keep in mind:

- State your position as clearly as you can.
- Be kind but firm.
- Don't expect the other person to agree with you.
- Be willing to hear the other person's point of view.
- Don't be afraid to repeat yourself, kindly but firmly.
- Don't attack or criticize the other person. (Stick to the matter at hand.)
- Stay in your own business.
- You are responsible for your opinion and feelings about the matter.

- The other person is responsible for his/her opinion and feelings about the matter.
- You don't need to offer explanations or excuses for your choices, opinions or behavior.
- Show the other person you hear what they are saying.
- Don't make the other person wrong just because he/she doesn't agree with you.
- Don't make yourself wrong (or criticize or excuse yourself).
- Remember, you don't need to agree with the other person to find a workable compromise.

Things you can say

When you are having this kind of discussion, here are some good ways to acknowledge the other person's point of view while maintaining your own rights, position, and point of view. You can say things like:

- I can understand how you might feel that way and I prefer...
- You could be right and I would rather...
- I can understand your point of view and I believe...
- I really appreciate your feelings (point of view) in this matter and I think...
- I agree with much of what you are saying and I prefer...
- I can sympathize with what you are saying and I would rather...
- I appreciate your thinking of me and the answer is still no.

Asking for what you want

Another side of being assertive is to learn to ask for what you want. You have the right to be you and to want what you want. People who are assertive understand this and are not afraid to ask for what they want. They are clear that the worst thing that can happen if they ask for what they want is a "no"! As a result, it's not so dangerous to ask for what you want when you understand this.

People who are non-assertive are often afraid to ask for what they want. So instead they try to get what they want by trying to manipulate other people. What do I mean by manipulating? I mean situations where one person is trying to get another person to do something they want by trying to make the other person feel guilty. Or by appealing to some arbitrary code of behavior or so-called norm instead of just asking straight out for what they want.

If you are in doubt about manipulation, you can be pretty sure someone is trying to manipulate you if instead of asking you directly for what he or she wants, the other person is trying to get you to do what they want by trying to make you feel guilty, anxious, or ignorant. If you look closely, you will see they are probably doing this by appealing to some 'higher' code of right and wrong that you are supposed to know about but apparently don't! This type of behavior occurs because we haven't learned to be assertive and simply ask for what we want. One of the areas where this can be a big problem is in our relationships.

Don't manipulate others – ask for what you want!

Arbitrary codes of behavior

People have all kinds of arbitrary rules and codes of behavior when it comes to the way things 'should' be done in relationships. As a result, we may get into trouble with our partners because we have somehow unknowingly violated one of their arbitrary codes of behavior or rules. Codes and arbitrary rules, which we weren't aware of to begin with – and which we might not agree with if we were aware of them! The list of unspoken, unwritten arbitrary rules that people have and use to try to manipulate and control each other is unfortunately rather long. This is why it is so important to try to uncover these belief systems and arbitrary rules and investigate them since they are motivating so much of our behavior. When we get a little clarity about these issues, a lot of unnecessary disagreement and drama can be avoided.

Negative inquiry

When you feel someone is trying to manipulate you, a good way to avoid being manipulated and uncover what's really going on is negative inquiry. When you use negative inquiry, it means that instead of getting defensive when the other person tries to manipulate you or make you feel guilty, you respond by asking questions.

Here's an example of how negative inquiry works. Let's say you want to spend some time alone this weekend. Your partner is upset because you want to spend time alone this weekend and tries to manipulate you by making you feel guilty for wanting what you want. Using negative inquiry, you can respond to his/her criticism with questions such as:

- I don't understand why my wanting to spend some time alone is making you unhappy.
- What is wrong with me wanting to spend some time alone this weekend?
- I don't understand why something like this upsets you?
- Why does my wanting to spend some time alone this weekend make you unhappy?
- I hear what you are saying, but why does my wanting to spend time alone upset you?

When you ask questions like this, you prompt the other person to explain why they are feeling as they do. When he or she answers, you may discover, for example, that your partner feels insecure when this situation arises because he/she equates your wanting to be alone with not loving him or her. This uninvestigated belief may be causing your partner a lot of anguish about something, which is just not true. You do love your partner and you still want to spend some time alone. In your mind, these two things are not connected; but in your partner's mind they are. As a result, a misunderstanding has arisen. By means of negative inquiry, you can bring this belief to light and hopefully clear up the misunderstanding. You can assure your partner that you really do love him/her and still want to have some time alone!

Another spin on the above scenario could be that your partner thinks that since you are a couple, you 'should' spend all your free time together. But who says people who are in love should spend all their free time together? Again, this is another interesting belief that may be causing a lot of anguish in a relationship. Regardless of what your negative inquiry uncovers, bringing uninvestigated beliefs out in the open can be a great help and clear up misunderstandings.

> **If you don't want to be manipulated,
> don't manipulate others!**

Questioning arbitrary belief systems

We all have underlying or basic beliefs about life like the ones mentioned above that we are usually unaware of. But whether we are aware of these beliefs or not, they influence our behavior and reactions in all the situations of our life. That's why it's always a good idea to try to uncover and investigate these beliefs and see if they are true or not. Because if these beliefs are untrue and are mere fantasies or misunderstandings about the nature of life and reality, we are causing ourselves needless suffering. When we uncover and question these basic beliefs we can release ourselves from those that are untrue. Then we experience a new freedom, and peace and harmony in our minds and thus in our lives.

Making other people suffer

When it comes to honest communications, here's a basic belief that many people are having trouble with. It's the idea that we can actually make other people suffer or that other people can make us suffer. This belief is really a gem. You are experiencing it if you sometimes have the feeling (without knowing exactly why) that your choices and actions are making other people suffer. Or it may be the other way around and you may feel that someone else's choices and actions are making you suffer. We find this interesting idea behind so many of the problems that arise in our relationships with our partners, family and friends.

But let us ask ourselves if this is true? Is it true that we have the power to make other people suffer? Or that someone else has the power to make us suffer?

When we understand that we live in a mental universe and that everything we experience in our lives – *everything* – is a thought, we understand that all our experiences are nothing more (and nothing less) than our interpretation of events. No event or circumstance has any inherent value or meaning in and of itself (which becomes obvious when we notice that different people react differently to the exact same event or situation.) So we see that no event or circumstance in itself can affect us one way or the other because we can only experience our thoughts about events and circumstances.

It takes only a little investigation to discover that this is true. Let's take some examples.

Example 1: Your boyfriend breaks your dinner engagement.
You were supposed to go out to dinner with your boyfriend tonight. At four o'clock in the afternoon he calls to tell you his

boss wants him to work late and he simply cannot get away so he has to cancel the date. Does his decision make you suffer? That depends on how you interpret his decision because your interpretation determines your reaction.

So how do interpret this and react?

- You're disappointed but understand. And you tell him so.
- You get angry because this isn't the first time this has happened. You think he's a workaholic and that he feels his job is more important than his relationship with you. You wonder if you want to continue the relationship. (You suffer.)
- You're relieved because you also have a lot of work piling up and you could use the evening to catch up. And you tell him so.
- You're overjoyed because you're tired and really want to have an evening to yourself.
- You're happy because you want him to do what's right for him in all situations and you tell him so.

And so on. Of course there are many more ways you could react. But the point is, how you experience the broken dinner engagement depends completely and entirely on your thoughts – and not on the fact that he had to cancel. Whether you are sad (suffer) or neutral or overjoyed depends entirely on your way of looking at things. It has absolutely nothing to do with him.

This is why we can say nothing external can affect us.

Let's take another example.

Example 2: Your mother criticizes you for making poor choices in your life.

You make an important life decision like dropping out of school, changing your job, moving away or getting married and your mother criticizes you. She says you're making a big mistake and you're going to regret it. She says you're immature and never listen. She's upset and unhappy with your decision. Do her comments make you suffer? That depends on how you interpret what she says because your interpretation determines your reaction.

So how do interpret this and react?

- You immediately get defensive and feel that your mother will never understand you and you tell her so. You end up quarreling and slamming down the phone. You feel angry and upset all week. (You suffer).

- You wonder how come you are so unfortunate to have a mother who never understands you. All your friends' mothers are so much more understanding and supportive. But you don't say anything. When the conversation is over, you feel hurt and humiliated at having such a mother. It bothers you all week long. (You suffer).

- You listen to what she's saying and reply "Mother you might be right and I still feel this is the best course of action for me. But thanks for your concern." You are really touched by her concern and tell her so but you also feel a bit sad that your mother doesn't really understand your situation. But you accept that that's just the way it is.

- You laugh to yourself because you know your mother doesn't have a clue about you and your life, but you don't tell her so. You know she's just a little old lady who's trying her best to help you and who wants you to have a good life.

And so on. Again there are many more ways you could react to your mother's remarks. And again we see that your experience of your mother's advice (whether it makes you suffer or sad or not) depends completely on your thoughts about your mother and her role in your life. Your reaction has nothing to do with your mother, but rather is the result of your beliefs and stories about your mother and your relationship to her. The reality is that your mother is just telling you what she thinks – based on her beliefs about life!

Beliefs about mothers

Of course if the above mother exchange upsets you and makes you suffer, it may be because you have other underlying beliefs about mothers that you need to examine. Your beliefs about mothers could sound like this:

- Mothers should understand their children.
- Mothers should be supportive of their children no matter what they do.
- Mothers should always be kind, tolerant and loving.
- Mothers shouldn't get mixed up in their children's affairs.
- Mothers should let go of their children when they grow up.

If any of these statements ring true to you, it might be a good idea to take a closer look at them. Because when you do, you will probably find that reality is quite different than these beliefs. The reality is:

- Mothers often don't understand their children (even if they try).
  - Mothers probably don't even understand themselves.
  - Does anyone understand anyone?
  - Do children understand themselves?
  - Why should mothers understand their children?
  - Do children understand their mothers?
  - And so on...
- Mothers are often not supportive of what their children do. Again this is reality.
- Mothers aren't always kind, tolerant and loving.
- Mothers often do meddle in their children's affairs.
- Mothers often don't let go of their children when they grow up.

So the question is – are you causing yourself unnecessary grief (and suffering) in your relationship by arguing with reality? Do you have unrealistic expectations to life and mothers? Are you expecting your mother to be different than she is? Are you making yourself unhappy by setting up a totally unrealistic standard for mothers that no mother can live up to? And if that is true, how would your relationship be with your mother if you were more realistic about who she really is and her ability to understand and support you? Wouldn't you take better care of yourself if you "got real" about who your mother really is instead of fighting reality?

But let's go back to our ability to make other people happy or unhappy...

Making other people happy

The flip side of the belief that we can make other people suffer is the belief that we can make other people happy. This translates into thoughts like:

- I can make other people happy.
- My choices and actions can make other people happy.
- I am responsible for the happiness of others.

Is this true? Do our actions really have the power to make other people happy or unhappy? Let's go back to the conversation you just had with your mother. You just told her you were going to drop out of college or move to another city and start a new life and she criticizes you. She says you're making a big mistake and you're going to regret it. She says you're immature and never listen. She's upset and unhappy with your decision – and it's making her unhappy. But there are an infinite number of other ways she could have reacted to your decision, depending on her beliefs and outlook on life. She could have said:

- Why darling I'm so glad you finally decided to move away from this dump and go someplace interesting!
- I support whatever you do. If it's good for you, then it's good for me.
- Great darling, that is wonderful news! You will love living in New York.
- I understand my dear. I wouldn't want you to end up with such a boring life as mine!
- I don't care what you do!
- It's OK with me but your father will have a heart attack when he hears the news.
- You must follow your heart dear and if this feels right to you, then go for it.
- I always thought you'd be happier being a belly dancer than going to medical school.

So what does your mother's reaction have to do with you? Her reaction is completely arbitrary and totally based on her beliefs about the world. In fact, she is just telling you her story of what she thinks the good life is. And if your actions make her happy – fine! It's still her story. (She was the one who made her happy – not you!)

Explaining your behavior

If you are trapped by the belief that somehow in some universe, you and your choices and actions can make other people happy, you end up getting stuck with the crazy idea that you are responsible for other people's happiness. Which is a cruel trick to play on yourself. It's especially cruel because when you have this belief, you then allow other people to ruthlessly manipulate your behavior without being aware of what's going on. Quite simply, it makes you a sitting duck... because it puts you in the terrible position of believing that you always have to explain your behavior, feelings and choices to other people. So no matter what you do, you feel you will be up for scrutiny if you fail to please someone. And all this comes from your sincere (but uninvestigated) belief that you somehow have the power to make other people happy or unhappy. As a result, you end up always explaining yourself – also to yourself – when you somehow fail to make other people happy.

What an impossible situation to put yourself in! This is definitely not the way to live a happy life! This I can tell you from experience. I tortured myself for years thinking my own dramatic decision to run away from home because of the Vietnam War (see the start of Chapter No. 7 for the story) when I was a teenager was the cause of so much unhappiness in my family because that is what my family told me, over and over again. It was like a broken record... how unhappy I'd made them, how much they'd suffered because of my choices, etc. etc. It was bloody hell. At the time, I didn't realize I came from a dysfunctional family and that trying to make other people responsible for their happiness is one of many confused things people do in dysfunctional families. In my case, it took me years to get over the guilt I felt. In fact it wasn't until I understood that I wasn't responsible for my parents' happiness (they were), that I realized it was their decision to blame me for not living up to their expectations, not mine. It was their interpretation of my actions that was making them unhappy, not me. I did what I believed was the right thing, not because I thought it would make them happy or unhappy. In reality, my choices and actions had nothing whatsoever to do with making them happy or unhappy. I did what I did for completely other reasons. Their reaction to my decision was their business; their unhappiness was the result of their beliefs.

The right to exist

Investigating this idea – that I should be able to explain myself – made me realize that this idea was actually threatening my very existence! I realized that when I thought I should be able to explain or justify my behavior, I felt that if I couldn't logically (whatever that means) explain or justify myself or my preferences to the people who were questioning me and my choices, I had no right to exist. Basically because if I couldn't explain myself to their satisfaction, I felt I had no right to be here and thus the whole basis of my existence came into question. I really and truly believed I should be able to justify my very existence on the planet. It was terrible and a totally hopeless task because explaining myself to someone else's satisfaction always meant trying to figure out what their belief system was and then squeezing myself into that system. And that was impossible. It was always a disaster and I always ended up being the loser! And feeling that I didn't have the right to exist at all since being me didn't fit into their system of right or wrong – whatever that was.

Of course at the time, I didn't realize that everyone was operating out of his or her own completely arbitrary system of right and wrong, so I was really trapped!

It was first when I began to understand the way the mind works and how these arbitrary belief systems influence us that I was able to set myself free. When I understood the mechanism I realized that no one can justify their existence. The whole idea is ridiculous. We just are here. And this doesn't mean that we are not accountable as I said before. We most definitely are. But that's not the same as having to explain yourself to someone else's satis-faction. Accountability is the law of the universe. And no one escapes the law. The law of cause and effect says everything we think, say and do has consequences. So your choices and actions always have consequences. The real question is – are you awake? Are you present? Are you aware of what you're thinking, saying, doing? That's the real question. Are you awake? What's your intention? Direction? Goal?

Set yourself free

If any of the above makes sense to you, then set yourself free. Allow yourself the freedom that is your birthright – the right to be you (and accept the consequences)! Ask yourself where you are not allowing yourself to be free – and set yourself free. Give up the impossible task of trying to explain yourself to other people when they are displeased. Stand up for yourself and your right to be you. Learn to be assertive.

If you want to go mountain climbing, do what it takes to go mountain climbing and accept the consequences. If you want to stay home and not go anywhere, stand up for your right to stay home and accept the consequences. Every choice has consequences, but you have the right to make your own decisions regardless of what anyone says. Don't let your own mistaken ideas about what you should or shouldn't do (according to whom?) rob you of your freedom. Stand up for yourself and your right to be you. Defend yourself and learn to deal with the criticism that goes with the turf of being you and living an authentic life.

Dealing with criticism

So how do we deal with criticism? And what in fact is criticism? According to Webster's Dictionary, to criticize is: "to judge or discuss the merits and faults of…" If you think about it carefully, you will discover that criticism is basically just one person telling another person what they think about a situation, event or person. So when someone criticizes you, he or she is really just telling you their beliefs about how they think things should be. As far as I can see, what we call criticism is just someone else's opinion. And when their opinion doesn't agree with ours we call it criticism. But basically, what they're doing is just telling us what they think about something. What they are saying may or may not be true. And that's about all there is to it.

But the way we react to criticism, well that's something

entirely different!

I used to find dealing with criticism extremely challenging so I have spent a lot of time exploring what criticism is and how we react to it. In my exploration, I discovered that when someone criticizes you, there are in fact only three ways of reacting.

Here's what I mean.

Let's take a simple example. Someone says to you: "You are an elephant." You can respond to this statement in three ways:

1. You can agree: Yes it's true. You've looked at yourself and you can see that yes it's true, you are an elephant. So you're not upset about the statement because you are clear about what is true for you.

2. You can disagree: No it's not true. You've looked carefully at yourself and you are sure that you are not an elephant. So again, you're not upset about the statement because you are clear about what is true for you. You know you are not an elephant; it's as simple as that. If someone else wants to think you're an elephant, well that's their business.

3. You get defensive and feel upset. Getting defensive and feeling upset is always a warning bell which is actually telling you that you yourself are unclear about the matter. You haven't really looked at the issue, so you're not sure yourself if you are an elephant or not. So when someone says you're an elephant, you feel discomfort, get defensive and upset and react by feeling or saying things like... 'How could she say that about me? He hurt my feelings. She doesn't love me. He doesn't understand. That was unkind.' When you react like this to criticism, it's a sure sign you are not clear as to what's true for you. So your reaction is telling you that you need to investigate this area of your life. In this case, it would be a sign that you need to take a closer look at yourself and find out if

you're really an elephant or not. Once you have investigated the statement, you will stop being defensive about it because you will know if it's true for you or not. And then when someone says you're an elephant, you experience only peace because you know whether or not you're an elephant. There's no mystery here.

When we understand that we can only react in these three ways – and why, we become less afraid of criticism. And we discover that in fact criticism is a gift – an opportunity for growth! Because if we're confused, it gives us the chance to become clear in yet another area of our lives – an area we haven't yet taken the time to investigate. Now we can find out what's true for us.

This understanding can be difficult to accept at first, but once you get the hang of it, you find out that criticism can be one of our best teachers (though maybe not always the most pleasant!).

The fear of making mistakes

Over the years, another one of the things my mother said to me countless times was, "Barbara you've made so many mistakes in your life." For years, I got upset when she said this because first of all I wasn't assertive enough to tell her to mind her own business and secondly because I didn't know what I really thought about this statement. Was it true that I'd made so many mistakes? Then as I gained new tools and deeper insight into myself and into dealing with people and criticism, I found that I was ready to explore what my mother was actually saying for myself. I wanted to find out if it was true or not. As soon as I started to look at the issue clinically, I found that before I could do anything, I had to define what the word 'mistake' meant. As soon as I held up the word 'mistake' to the light of inquiry, I discovered that my mother was using the word 'mistake' as a way of saying she didn't approve of my choices or actions. Because what is a mistake? Webster's Dictionary says a mistake is 'an error in action or judgment'. But according to whom? When an error in action or judgment is made, it must be in relation to some system of right and wrong or in relation to some rules and regulations. That made me realize that obviously my mother's idea of what a mistake is was based on her belief system and on her ideas of good and bad/right and wrong.

Further investigation made me realize that in reality there are only actions and the consequences of these actions. And that's all there is, in reality. There is no such thing as a 'mistake'. A mistake is in fact impossible. We make decisions or choices and then our action or activity has a consequence or consequences. The word 'mistake' only comes into play when we talk about our interpretation or evaluation of an action and its consequences. If you 'like' the consequences of a certain action, you may believe a good choice was made, if you dislike the consequences of a certain action, you may believe a mistake was made. There's nothing more to it.

So I discovered, in my mother's case, that she disliked the fact that I protested against the Vietnam war, dropped out of college, ran away from home, traveled the world, took drugs, became a hippy, settled in a foreign country, became a Macrobiotic teacher, then turned into a spiritual seeker, consciousness explorer and teacher, and didn't marry a doctor and didn't settle down in suburbia USA. When I examined what was going on, I found out this was her definition of 'making mistakes'. So when she said I made a lot of mistakes, besides minding my business, she was actually telling me (rather unskillfully) that from her point of view I did not make choices, which would have led to what she considered a good life. In her view, a good life meant marrying a man who was preferably a doctor or a lawyer and who had money and then spending the rest of my life living in a nice house in suburbia USA. So yes, in her eyes, my choices were 'mistakes'. That was her story and she got to live it, while I went on my merry way and had my own very exciting and happy life!

In my consideration of this concept of 'making a mistake' I began to notice that lots of other people are also afraid of the idea of making mistakes. And I started to ask myself why is this so? What is it about the idea of making mistakes that strikes such terror in our hearts? When I explored this issue for myself, I discovered that for me, the fear of making mistakes was based on the idea that life is serious business and that since life is such serious business, it was dangerous to make a so-called mistake. My thinking went something like this, well if you make a mistake, you'll find yourself in a situation you'll never be able to get out of, or you'll be screwed for the rest of your life (whatever that meant), or you'll be punished – not that I really knew what I meant by the idea of being punished. The other thing that I connected to the idea of making a mistake was the idea that if I made a mistake, it was a sure sign that I was not OK. I think the logic went something like this – if you're OK, you just don't make mistakes! But again all of these uninvestigated thoughts were based on the idea that some actions and activities were right and some were wrong. Which lead me back to the… 'according to whom' question. And when you get to the 'according to whom' question, you discover (to your everlasting relief) that it's all relative and that a mistake can only be defined in a certain context. In other words, you can only believe that you made a mistake if you buy the arbitrary belief system (and all belief systems are arbitrary) that says this is 'wrong' and that is 'right'. When you drop the belief systems and the value judgments, you find out there is no such thing as a 'mistake'. It's just not possible. All that is left, as I said before, is an action and a consequence. In other words, you do something and something else happens as a result. And that's about it. And the great part of it all is that no matter what happens, we always have the opportunity to look at what's going on and learn. That's the true beauty of life, the fact that it offers us endless opportunities to explore and grow. And it's fun (and not serious business) too!

No. 4

Investigate your stories

> **The number 4 cause of suffering and unhappiness are the scary stories you tell yourself about life and the world.**

Have you ever almost scared yourself to death about something that never happened? Or gotten yourself into a panic about something you thought just might happen one day but never did? Or told yourself stories about the potential negative outcome of events that were far off in the future? Or fantasized about what you'd do if lost your job or got a terminal illness? Or invented worst-case scenarios that played out like Hollywood catastrophe films? Well if you have or do, welcome to the club! Because you're not alone. You see the worry club is probably the biggest club on the planet. Almost everyone is a member, at least everyone I know is! Although I have heard of a few wise souls who seem to have dropped out of the club. But they are few and far between indeed.

Of course the worry club has different levels of membership. Some worriers practice daily and are true experts, while others only use their worrying skills on special occasions! But all in all, it's the most extraordinary club, because it's a totally useless association, which does no one any good. Just think about it for a moment and look back at your life. Five years ago weren't you worrying about pretty much the same things as you worry about today? Weren't you worrying about your health or your finances or your kids or your relationship? And look at you today. You're still here and you're still probably worrying about the same things – despite all your past worrying! And what happened? The truth is probably nothing much happened did it? OK maybe there was a bump in the road here and there, but not much else. And if something really 'serious' did happen, it almost certainly wasn't what you were worrying about in the first place. It was probably something completely different, something you weren't expecting at all. But still you managed to get here, despite all your worrying and the bumps in the road! So the question is, did all that worrying help at all? Did it make the passage from then to now any easier? The honest answer for all of us is probably not. The honest answer is that worrying doesn't make the journey through life one bit easier. Quite the contrary, it just wears us out unnecessarily! I know it's true for me. When I think of all the wear and tear I could have saved myself if I hadn't worried so much! I worried and worried and what happened? The years passed and I got older, but I'm still here and still pretty much OK.

Can we just stop?

No we can't. Not just like that. We all know it doesn't work to tell ourselves to stop worrying. If you're anything like me, you've probably tried countless times to stop worrying only to discover it just doesn't work. We tell ourselves over and over again not to worry and then we still worry! Even though we know that worrying is negative, stupid, stressful, and a total waste of time – and that nothing good ever comes from it.

So what can we do?

Is there a way to stop that works?

In my experience, there's only one way to deal with worrying – and that's to shine the light of truth on the things we are worrying about. Instead of suppressing or running away from the thoughts that are worrying us, I've discovered that the best way to deal with them is to examine them and find out if they're true. Why? Because if we discover we're worrying about things that are really not true, it makes it much more difficult to keep on worrying about them!

Typical worry scenarios

But let's look at some of our worries first. I've discovered that we all worry about pretty much the same things and tell ourselves very similar stories. No one is special; we're all in the same boat. Of course there are variations on our major themes, but we all basically worry about the same things. One of our main worry themes is our health. We worry about life in these physical bodies and about the maintenance and upkeep of physical life in these bodies. We worry about how we feel and how we look. We worry about our aches and pains. We worry about growing old. In other words, a lot of our worries – maybe most of our worries – are connected to these bodies. Sometimes when I'm really worried about my health, I think that if I didn't have this body, I'd have absolutely nothing to worry about! No body = no worries! But since we do have bodies, most of us worry about them.

We also worry about survival while we're in these bodies, so we worry about money and our jobs and our financial security. And we worry about how our body is getting along with other bodies, so we worry about our relationships or about being alone.

But whatever we're worrying about, you will find when you examine it, that it is some kind of scary story we are telling ourselves about what might happen to life in this body. Here are some of the main ones:

- If I get sick, I won't be able to manage.
- Life is dangerous and the world is a scary place.
- There is something wrong with me.
- There's something wrong with what I want.
- I am not OK.
- I should be in control.

- If something happens to my child, I'll be devastated.
- If I do what I want, he/she won't like/love me anymore.
- I'll end up all alone.
- Something bad will happen to me and I'll be dependent on others.
- If my partner leaves, I'll be lonely.
- Being sick or in pain is unfair. (It's unfair that I should suffer so.)
- Without money, there's no security.
- Something might go wrong.
- And so on...

Let's look more closely at a few of these scenarios we worry about so much. Because when we take a closer look, we find they are very juicy stories indeed!

If I get sick, I won't be able to manage.
Almost everyone worries about getting sick and not being able to manage. For some people, the slightest ache or pain can set them off on a rampage, imagining all the terrible things the future will bring. They see cancer, helplessness, and loneliness. They see being a burden on their family, ending up in a hospital and dying all alone... This story is a great way to worry yourself sick.

Life is dangerous and the world is a scary place.
This is another one of those juicy stories we tell ourselves. We probably learned this one from our parents and the media does everything in its power to give us more fuel for the fire! We're also experts at passing on this story to our kids. (See the section 'Is life dangerous' in Chapter No. 10 for a closer look at this thought.)

I'll be lonely without a partner.
Are you staying in an unsatisfactory relationship because you are

afraid of being alone? Are you making yourself sick by telling yourself the story of how lonely you will be if you leave your partner or if he/she leaves you?

There is something wrong with what I want.
Here's another good story you might be telling yourself when you can't explain or justify the way you are – or your choices and behavior – to the people close to you.

There is something wrong with me.
Another juicy spin on the one above – which gives us endless heartache!

I should be in control.
Here's another superb story that most of us have despite the fact that everything in the whole universe is spinning along perfectly without our doing anything at all! No wonder we feel crazy when we tell ourselves this story – we're asking ourselves to do the impossible.

If you're nodding your head and saying yes, that sounds like me – what do you do next? My answer is – investigate your stories and your worries. Hold them up to the light of truth and see if there is any truth to them. OK you say, but how do I do that?

Byron Katie and "The Work"

The best modern-day tool I know to investigate our stories with is "The Work of Byron Katie". The Work comprises four simple questions that any of us can use to examine our fears, worries and stories and see whether or not they are true.

The interesting thing about doing The Work is that when you ask the four questions and find your own truth, many of your worries just disappear. It's amazing. Somehow when you discover for yourself that one of your scary stories simply isn't true, it no longer has such a hold over you and it dissolves all by itself. So instead of trying to stop worrying, you just do.

The other interesting thing about The Work is that it's really a modern version of the traditional inquiry techniques that many of the great teachers have taught throughout the ages. So many teachers have said find out what is truth because only the truth will set you free. But the trouble is, we don't really know how to do this. We don't know how to find out what our truth is. Now Byron Katie offers us four questions that really cut through all the confusion to the heart of the matter, quickly and effectively. And you don't need any special training to use the questions. You can do it by yourself or with your partner or friends.

The four questions of The Work of Byron Katie are:

1. Is it true?
2. Can you absolutely know that it's true?
3. How do you react when you think that thought?
4. Who would you be without the thought?
and
The turnaround (the exact opposite of the original statement).

From Byron Katie's book *Loving What Is*

Does this sound too easy to be true? Ok, well let's try the four questions on one of the above statements and see what happens. Let's take the first one:

If I get sick, I won't be able to manage.

1. Is it true? "Well yes, if I get sick. I won't be able to manage because I won't be able to go to work and then how will I pay my bills, etc. I'll lose my house and end up on welfare or in an institution."

2. Can you absolutely know that it's true? "Well no. I can't absolutely know it's true. I have been sick before and managed to keep my job. I was on sick leave and then I got better and things worked out. And if I really got sick my kids or my parents would probably help me or my friends would, and there is government help too. So no I can't absolutely know that I wouldn't be able to manage if I get sick."

3. How do you react when you think that thought *if I get sick, I won't be able to manage*? "It makes me feel terrible. I get so worried and upset when I don't feel well and then I feel that my whole existence depends on me having good health. It's terrible; it makes me so tense and afraid all the time."

4. Who would you be without the thought? Who would you be if you couldn't think the thought that *if I get sick I won't be able to manage...*? "Well I would be a lot happier and so much more relaxed. I wouldn't worry so much about my future and I would enjoy my life right now much more."

The turnaround. What is the exact opposite of the original statement? It could be: *If I get sick, I will be able to manage.* Is this statement as true or truer than your original statement? "Well yes, I can see that this could be as true or truer than my original statement because in reality when I've been sick before I have managed."

What happens next? If you allow yourself to go through this exercise very slowly and mindfully and give yourself the time to sit with each question and listen to your own inner voice and your own answers, you will begin to see how your own thoughts are making you suffer. You will see how much anguish your stories are actually causing you because when you examine them, you discover that in reality, nothing has actually happened. You're worrying about a dream, a fantasy! In the above story, for example, you discovered that the reality is that when you got sick previously, things worked themselves out just fine and it wasn't so terrible as you are imagining it could be. Then we find that question 4 'Who would you be without the thought' and the 'turnaround' allow you to explore how it feels not to identify so strongly with your original worry thought. When you do this, you discover that your scary projections about the future just dissolve in the light of truth and you can relax and enjoy this now moment.

The truth is so energizing!

(See Byron Katie's books *Loving What Is* and *I Need Your Love – Is That True?* for a detailed explanation of the four questions and how to do The Work.)

Unhappy now?

Besides our worry thoughts about the future, there is another type of story we are telling ourselves which gives us a lot of anguish. These are the stories about what is preventing us from being happy in this now moment. The 'if only' stories, which often sound like this: 'If only he'd listen, I'd be happy. If only the sun was shining, I'd be happy. If only my back didn't hurt, I'd be happy. If only I had a little more money in the bank, I'd be happy. If only I'd gotten that promotion, I'd be happy, If only he loved me, I'd be happy...' you know the drill.

When you find yourself telling stories like these, it's another brilliant opportunity to use the four questions. You can even do it as a game or fun exercise. Start by identifying the stories you are telling yourself about what's keeping you from being happy at this very moment. I know I asked this question before, but this time I'd like you to be very specific and write down exactly what's preventing you from being happy right now – and then ask the four questions about these statements.

Think about this carefully and write it down. What's keeping you from being happy right now? Is it your job? Is it your boss at work? If that's what it is, what's the story? Write it down. Is it your health? If it is, what's the story? Is it your relationship with your partner or your children? If it is, what's the story? Is it the weather? Is it your age, your looks, the amount of money in your bank account? What exactly is preventing you from being happy right now? Is it the world situation? Is it your father's health? What is it? Pinpoint the story and write it down. Then ask the four questions about each of your statements.

In my experience, when you ask the four questions and investigate what is preventing you from being happy at this moment, the stories often dissolve in the light of truth. And when this happens, happiness appears automatically. You don't have to 'do' anything to make yourself happy. In fact you can't. What you find instead is that you are just happy because you are happiness itself. Happiness is your nature.

> **You don't see the world as it is –**
> **you see the world as you are.**

A mental universe

We live in a mental universe and that means that nothing but our thoughts can prevent us from being happy right now. No event or outside circumstance can do this, only a story. But please don't believe me; find out for yourself if this radical claim is true.

And there's only one way to do this and that's to try what I'm suggesting. Write down everything that is preventing you from being happy right now and investigate your stories. Find out what's true. If you go to a psychologist, she will ask you to tell your stories. If you go to a doctor, she will ask you to tell your stories. If you go to your friend, she will ask you to tell your stories. Everyone wants to know your stories, but the best teachers and friends are the ones who can help you investigate your stories and find out if they are true or not. So ask the four questions and set yourself free.

When you have written down your stories and asked the four questions, you will have uncovered your own delusion! The delusion that is preventing you from being happy now. Why do I say this? Ask the four questions and find out for yourself! Find out if there is anything, anything at all in this whole universe that is preventing you from being happy at this now moment.

I know this is a very ambitious claim, but it's true nevertheless. When you follow the guidelines in this book and examine your stories, you will discover for yourself that this is true. You will discover there is always – *always* – a story that is preventing you from being happy right now. Why is that so? Because as I just said, we live in a mental universe. All our experiences are determined by our thoughts. Nothing else is going on – and that's the good news – because it means that nothing – absolutely nothing but our thoughts can prevent us from living a happy life right now. Nothing else, no outside event or circumstance can do this, only our stories can do this. But please don't believe me; find out for yourself if this is true.

A third kind of storytelling

There's another kind of storytelling that can be veiling your happiness like a cloud and that's the negative kind of storytelling that involves dwelling on past grudges and reliving past hurts.

No matter how much someone or something hurt in the past, by retelling the story in the present, it's still happening now, it's still your experience now, at this very moment. The unhappiness you are feeling is now. Just like when we worry about the future, your anguish is happening now. All our experiences are still happening right here and now. There is no place else they can happen and this is obviously because there is only the now. The past and the future do not exist; they are only thoughts in our mind, which are happening now. So your story, whatever it is, is also still happening now. Of course this is equally true of our positive storytelling, i.e., our pleasant memories and happy anticipations. They too are present thoughts; they too are our experiences now. But since happy memories and pleasant anticipations are happy thoughts, we don't need to investigate them! But in trying to clear your mind and remove the clouds that are blocking the experience of your own true happy nature, you might want to consider how dwelling on past hurts is influencing you now. When you dwell on past hurts, how does it make you feel right now and how does this influence your present choices and behavior?

A good way to do this is to go through your so-called life story in as much detail as you can and when you find areas of discomfort, write them down. Write down the story of the events that are bothering you and then investigate them by asking Byron Katie's four questions. And see what happens!

What about memory?

But what about memory and the role of memory in all this? I bring this up now because your reaction to what I'm saying may be… but I remember… "When he left me, I was devastated." Or "When she stole my money, I was furious because I had to start all over." "When our business went bankrupt, I was so depressed that I had a nervous breakdown." "When my father died, I cried for weeks."

When we look at these statements, it is interesting to note that there are two pieces of information in each statement. There is our memory of the actual events, the so-called facts, which includes the first part of each of the above statements: "He left me." "She stole my money." "We went bankrupt." "My father died." These are the facts. This is memory of events, of the things that happened.

But then there is the second part of each statement or memory – which is the story we attach to the events. This type of memory is our interpretation of the things that happen to us. Our stories are our way of telling us what these events mean, and each story is based on our beliefs about life. So we say, "When he left me, I was devastated." "When she stole my money, I was furious because I had to start all over." "When the business went bankrupt, I was so depressed that I had a nervous breakdown." "When my father died, I cried for weeks." In each case, we can see we combined the event with our interpretation of the event and came out with a story.

- *When he left me, I was devastated.* This story could be based on beliefs like:
  - It's terrible to be alone.
  - People should stay together when they are married.
  - I can't manage on my own.
  - I need his love.
- *When she stole my money, I was furious because I had to start all over.* This story could be based on beliefs like:
  - People should be honest. (People shouldn't steal.)
  - Having to start all over is unfair.
  - She had no right to my money.
  - She was a greedy bitch who just wanted my money.
- *When the business when bankrupt, I was so depressed that I had a nervous breakdown.* This story could be based on beliefs like:
  - Businesses shouldn't go bankrupt.
  - Bankruptcy is bad.
  - It's impossible to be happy without financial security.
  - I need business success to be happy.
- *When my father died, I cried for weeks.* This story could be based on beliefs like:
  - My father should have lived forever.
  - Death is cruel.
  - I can't manage without my father's love and support.
  - My father shouldn't have suffered so much.

Looking at examples like the above, it becomes clear that when things happen in our lives, we attach storylines to these events based on our beliefs about life. Then when we remember these events, they have specific meanings for us – and a certain emotional charge. This is something we are doing all the time, all our lives. And there's nothing basically wrong with doing this except if our stories are making us suffer and are preventing us from living happy lives.

If this is the case, if our stories and memories are causing discomfort, anguish and distress, then it can be a good idea to take a closer look at these stories and the beliefs behind the stories, and ask Byron Katie's four questions.

> **Identification with our thoughts makes us suffer.**
> **There is no other suffering.**

Can outside circumstances affect me?

When you start to investigate your stories you discover that in every case there is an event and then there is your interpretation of the event as described above. But there's another thing that eventually dawns on us as we begin to explore and play with these concepts – and that is that *the only thing that can affect us is our thoughts*. All events, regardless of what they are, are neutral. They have no meaning in and of themselves, however radical this statement may sound. This is the way it is.

The truth is things just happen. Our experience of events is a result of our beliefs and our interpretation of whether these happenings are good or bad, happy or sad, right or wrong, etc. That is all we are experiencing. All we are experiencing is our interpretation of the meaning of these events. That is all that can happen. And that is our life; that is our world. Nothing else is going on. (Nothing else can go on.)

So if we believe an event is bad, that is our experience.

If we believe an event is good, that is our experience.

And even more basically, if we believe that outside events, circumstances and people can influence us – then they can! I know this is getting tricky, but it's rather like the placebo effect. If you believe the pill will take away your headache, then it will, even if it's just a sugar tablet! The same goes for everything else in life.

You get what you believe.

So it really comes down to this: Events can only affect you if you think they can! But the truth is… nothing can affect you but your own thoughts! I find this so radical and so amazing, that the implications of this continue to fascinate me… and this is what it leaves me with:

It's only my thought that something can affect me – that can affect me!

It's only my thought that other people can affect me – that can affect me!

It's only my thought that the weather can affect me – that can affect me!

It's only my thought that you can affect me – that can affect me!

It's only my thought that my body can affect me – that can affect me!

It's only my thought that outside forces can affect me – that can affect me!

**Events can only affect you if you think they can.
You get what you believe.**

It's like we're collective sleepwalkers who don't see this! Collective sleepwalkers who are walking around in the dream that other people, events, things and circumstances have power over us, when in fact they don't! It's a collective lie that we've all swallowed and until we wake up we'll suffer just the way we believe we should suffer! It's all so perfectly tuned and timed, the square is so perfectly round, the dream is so perfectly real... but the truth is, it isn't! Nothing is real except your thoughts. (And even your thoughts are not real – because what are thoughts? Thoughts are just thoughts. And nobody has ever pinned down a thought!)

The truth is you are all there is and your thoughts are your entire experience. There is nothing else going on. Take away thought and what do you have? What experience is left? It's a mind-boggling thought.

And there we have it...

Thoughts arising, world arising.

Your thoughts arising, your world arising.

And that's about it.

(If this idea frightens you, it's because you don't understand it yet. The truth is, this is the key to absolute freedom.)

So if you want absolute freedom, which is true happiness, wake yourself up and play with these ideas until they click for you! Only you can do this, no one else can do it for you – and once you get it, no one else can take it from you.

He's an energy drainer

In light of the above we can ask ourselves all kinds of interesting questions about our previous beliefs. Here's a good one – is it true that other people can drain our energy? I ask this question because being an energy drainer is one of those popular stories I often hear floating around. People say things like, "Oh he's such an energy drainer." Or "I don't like to be with her because she drains my energy." Or "My mother is a real energy drainer." Or "Being with her really brings me down." But is it true? Can other people bring us down and drain our energy? And if they can, how do they actually do this? What is the mechanism? When I asked one woman I know to explain this phenomenon to me, she actually put her hand up to her neck to show me how an energy drainer puts his or her energy-draining tube right into her neck and draws out her energy! It was exciting to see. What a belief to have! It must make life seem very dangerous because you never know when you're going to meet someone who is going to stick their energy-draining tube right into you and suck you dry!

But if nothing can affect us but our own thoughts, how is this possible? How can someone drain our energy? So what is really going on when we say we feel drained after being with someone? What can possibly drain us and make us feel tired except our own thoughts about a person or situation? Interesting isn't it!

The woman with multiple sclerosis

Here's another one: My friend Dorothy is in her late 50s and has multiple sclerosis. Once Dorothy was married and she now has two grown children and she's a grandmother. Today Dorothy is confined to a wheelchair. She cannot get up by herself or walk or go to the bathroom or get dressed or use her hands (even to hold a book for more than a few minutes). She lives in a special apartment and has round-the-clock assistance from the social health services. Someone comes and gets her out of bed, puts her on the toilet, washes her, gets her dressed, puts her in a wheelchair. Another person comes with food and feeds her. Another comes and takes her clothes off in the evening and puts her back to bed. Sometimes someone comes and takes her out in her wheelchair – for a drive or to some event.

In light of the above, we can ask ourselves… can Dorothy have a happy life or does the fact that she has multiple sclerosis and is so handicapped mean she can't? She has exactly the same mind/consciousness as everyone else. And if nothing can influence her experience except her own thoughts… what is preventing Dorothy from having a happy life right now?

The Count of Monte Cristo

And what about the Count of Monte Cristo or the prisoners at Guantanamo Bay? Can they have happy lives? I like to test these concepts in so-called extreme situations because if they don't hold in extreme situations – then they don't hold at all. But if mind/consciousness is everything, they must.

Remember the Count of Monte Cristo? It is the incredible tale by Alexandre Dumas of Edmond Dantés who was framed and falsely imprisoned in the Chateau d'If on a lonely island in the Mediterranean for 14 years. Why is this tale so popular and so fascinating? Is it because we all wonder how we would fare if we found ourselves in such a situation? Solitary confinement for 14 years in a cell with nothing to do! Is it possible to live a happy life in these circumstances? And what about the prisoners at Guantanamo Bay? Can they have happy lives?

And how does this kind of isolation compare with the tales of Milarepa and the other great masters of Tibet who voluntarily went to the mountains and meditated for decades on their own in solitary caves, completely isolated from the world? They too were isolated, but the difference of course was that they went of their own free will. They wanted to be isolated from the world and from outside distractions. To them isolation was a happy thought, while for most prisoners, isolation is not a happy thought. But regardless of the thoughts, we're still looking at the same solitary existence. We're still looking at human beings doing the exact same things but having completely different experiences because they have different ideas about what these experiences and events mean.

I must admit I find it fascinating to ponder extreme situations like these in light of our original question – what determines whether people are living happy lives or not? Since we discover, when we investigate things, that each person's experience is totally and completely determined by his/her thoughts about what is happening to them, it makes me conclude over and over again that mind/consciousness is everything. And the determining factor in living a happy life!

> **If you can think yourself to unhappiness,
> you can un-think yourself to happiness.**

Mind your own business

> **The number 5 cause of suffering and unhappiness is minding other people's business.**

Minding other people's business is a surefire way to make yourself unhappy. That's why if you want to live a happy life, I highly recommend you take a close look at this mechanism and ask yourself whose business you are in?

But what exactly do I mean by "minding someone else's business"?

Well when you mind your own business, you take care of yourself. You are in your own space, focusing on what is going on inside you and on what's good for you. And you try to make the best possible decisions and take the best possible actions based on everything you know, feel, and love.

When you are minding someone else's business, you are in their space either telling the person in your mind or out loud to their face what you think they should feel, think and/or do. When you do this, you're minding their business. And minding another person's business is quite simply invading their space, unless they have specifically asked for your help or opinion.

So try watching yourself during the day and ask yourself "Whose business am I in right now? Am I minding my own business or someone else's? Who am I making judgments and decisions for right now? For me or for someone else? And who am I worrying about right now? Who am I thinking about, making plans for, or afraid for?"

You might want to put this book down and ask yourself this

question right now. Who's in your mind at the moment? Who are you worried about right now? Is it your mate, your parents, your friends, your kids? And what kind of worry is it? Is it concrete and practical because you're standing right next to this person and he or she is in a life and death situation right this minute and only you can save them? (Probably not because how can you be reading this book at the same time?) Or are you extending yourself into their space and making judgments and suggestions – in your own mind – that are not yours to make?

It's interesting to think about. And it's interesting to observe as you go through your day and interact with your family, friends and business colleagues. This is a new concept for many people because it's something we don't learn in school. So few people are truly aware of what they're doing. But if you want to live a happy life, the time to wake up and become aware of this mechanism is right now. The key to releasing yourself and others is to *stay at home in your own business*. Watch what you're doing and when you find you are moving out of your own space, make the conscious decision to pull back your ideas about what you think other people should or shouldn't be doing. And stay home with yourself!

Having healthy boundaries

When you mind your own business, it is a sign that you understand what it means to have healthy boundaries. When we have healthy boundaries, we understand that I am me and you are you and that each of us has a right to be here and to be who we are. It also means that each of us has the right to make choices for ourselves and then to experience the consequences of all our thoughts, words and actions. When we have healthy boundaries we understand this and respect everyone's right to be or do what feels right for them (and experience the consequences).

As a result of having healthy boundaries we respect other people's rights and we expect other people to respect our rights.

This means that when you tell someone how they should think or feel or what they should say or do when they don't specifically ask for your advice, you are not respecting their boundaries and their right to be them. And it works the other way too. Which means when someone tells you how you should think or feel or what you should say or do when you don't specifically ask them for their advice; they are not respecting your boundaries and your right to be you. Either way, these are examples of boundary violations and feel uncomfortable when they arise. So minding your own business means to respect other people and not tell them what to think, say or do unless they specifically ask for your advice or opinion.

When you start to understand this mechanism and begin to notice what you're doing, you're probably going to find that a lot of the time you're everywhere except at home with yourself. If this is the case, don't despair. Becoming aware of this mechanism is in itself a powerful impulse for transformation. And it works automatically because as you start to see what you are doing, your natural inclination will be to pull back your ideas and suggestions as to what you think is good for other people. Your natural inclination will be to let them decide for themselves. Because as you wake up, it becomes obvious that you can't know what's good for them anyway. In my experience, thinking that you can or do, causes nothing but pain and personal anguish.

So all we're left with is the question – whose business are you in? Theirs or yours?

Who's at home?

There's another thing about minding other people's business, and it's when you're out there minding someone else's business, who's at home minding yours?

It took me a lot of inner work to understand this mechanism, but when I got it, I found it was such a huge relief. Because it's truly liberating and energizing to bring yourself home to your own business – and to stop draining yourself mentally and emotionally by being in other people's business. But I admit, it takes practice to learn to stay home with yourself because being in other people's business is a bad mental habit. You get used to doing it (or at least I did), so you have to watch yourself if you want to kick the habit and rap yourself firmly over the knuckles every time you catch yourself being in someone else's business.

But again, awareness is the key.

Being a good person

When I tried to analyze why I spent so much time and energy minding other people's business, I discovered that it had to do with the mistaken idea that being a 'good person' means worrying about other people and trying to take care of them. I thought that if I was 'loving and kind' it meant I must do everything I possibly could to make other people happy. When I thought like this, I was always trying to 'second guess' what was going on in my partner's mind or in my kids' minds or in my friends' minds. Which I am sure made me a real drag to be with! And this mindset caused me a lot of anxiety too because no matter how hard I tried, it was impossible to get it right!

Are you like this too?

Feeling you have to know what everyone else is thinking, doing, and feeling? Feeling that if you want to be a good person you should be on top of every situation and figure out exactly what everyone else wants! But how can you? I mean in truth it's hard enough to just figure out what you want and what you're feeling about yourself, let alone other people! I mean how can we know? All I can say is I found trying to know what other people want all the time was and is a real nightmare and totally impossible. And what does it get you? In my experience it gets you nothing and nowhere – all it does is piss other people off. Big time. When you think about it, minding someone else's business is really the same as saying they don't have a mind of their own, that they don't have enough intelligence to take care of themselves and actually that's really insulting. I don't want other people to treat me like that, so what gives me the right to treat other people that way? Especially if it's someone I love like my children or partner. Now that I understand the mechanism, I see how truly ridiculous these beliefs and behavior are. Especially if we want to live happy, harmonious lives!

But the reality is, a lot of us are minding other people's businesses a lot of the time – instead of minding our own. Of course I'm not saying we should come down on ourselves like a ton of bricks because we've been behaving in ways that cause ourselves and other people discomfort. I'm just saying if you watch yourself and contemplate this mechanism you will become aware of what you're doing. And then your thinking and behavior will automatically adjust themselves. Awareness is the key because being in other people's business is just unconscious, automatic behavior you fall into because you haven't investigated your thinking. And this is especially true if you're a "people pleaser"!

Spot check

So during your day, do some spot checks. Stop up and ask yourself, "Whose business am I minding now? Am I staying in my own space or am I invading someone else's space?" And if you think you know what's best for someone else, ask yourself again, "Can I really know what's good for her?"

Once you begin to see what's going on, you will see how other people fall into this trap too. Parents, for example, are really great at this – to everyone's dismay. And of course it's not difficult to understand how parents can get stuck in this kind of behavior. It's a parents' job to take care of their children when they are small, but as a child grows up, the wise parent will give the child more and more space and be less and less in the child's business. This is wisdom's way. We all know this in our hearts.

Authority figures in general and grandparents and school-teachers are also experts at being in other people's business. But again, it's not difficult to understand why this behavior might develop considering their roles in society.

But if you want to live a happy life, it's wise to remember:

- Set everyone free in your mind
- Respect everyone's right to decide for themselves
- Let people do what they like (and experience the consequences)
- Don't be attached to what other people say or decide to do
- Don't be possessive of people or things
- Stop trying to make other people like or dislike what you like or dislike
- Bring yourself home to yourself
- Stay in your own space

In short, mind your own business!

What about parents and children?

But you say, what about parents who want to protect their children? What about parents who want to save their children from the troubles and hardships they believe they themselves have suffered? What is going on here? Of course as I said before, it's a parent's job to love and provide for their kids and give them food, clothing, shelter, and teach them to get along in the world to the best of their ability, because this is what we do as parents. This is the way of it. But as for protecting children from suffering, we need to ask ourselves if it is possible for one human being to protect another human being from suffering? We need to ask ourselves if it is possible for anyone to keep another person from their destiny path, which is life being lived through their own mind. And since life can only be lived through the mind that is living it, how can anyone prevent another mind from seeing and experiencing what it sees and experiences? Each one sees each experience through his/her own eyes. And even parents cannot know what the other is experiencing, ever. Even if the other is their very own child. Because this too is the way of it. Despite the bond of love and the closeness of parent-child, still we cannot know what the other sees, feels, touches, lives. So how can we know what is good for the other?

And here's another question. Parents often say they don't want their children to make the same 'mistakes' as they made. But we need to question this idea too. First of all, is it possible to make mistakes? As I said in Chapter No. 3, there is no such thing as a mistake. There are only actions and the consequences of these actions. A mistake is really just someone's negative interpretation of an action and its consequence. So if you don't like what happens, then it's a mistake. If you like what happens, well then it was a good choice. Nothing more is going on.

So why in heaven's name would we want to stop our children from acting and experiencing the consequences of their actions? How else can they learn? What else is there to do in life, but act and see the consequences? When this happens the heart grows wise, there is no other way. How did your wisdom come to you? Did you inherit it or was it the gift of life itself? Was it your very own seeing and experiencing that brought it to you? And would you want to deprive another human being of this precious experience – especially your own children?

And even if you do want to prevent your own children from living their very own lives, you will find it's impossible to do. Trying to prevent children from living and acting is like trying to stop the wind. It just doesn't work, fortunately for all of us. And fortunately for all of us, the way of it is that each one has his or her own full share of this thing called life – in whatever guise it comes to us. And nothing can prevent life from being lived through each of us. That fortunately is just the way of it. No matter how much people try to interfere!

Knowing what's best

As for knowing what is best – who are we to judge anyway? Who are we to know what is appropriate or inappropriate for another human being? Even if that human being is your child? Or especially if that human being is your child... Knowing what is best is definitely minding someone else's business! Knowing what is best is definitely interfering. So when you feel you know what is best – ask yourself – how can you possibly know what is best? Do you have the gift of prophecy? Can you see the end of all things?

Understanding this doesn't mean we cannot be there for our children, partners, and other people. Understanding this does not mean we cannot be supportive and loving, but this is not the same as interfering. We can be there if that's what someone else wants and we can speak truthfully if someone asks. When you are mindful, you understand the signals and then speaking truthfully could sound like this:

- I can understand that you might want to do that – and in my experience I found...
- I know that sounds like fun and in my experience...
- Try it and see what happens...
- When I was in a similar situation, this is what I did...
- That might be good for you, I don't know.
- In my experience, doing something like that leads to... but try it and see what happens...
- It didn't work for me, but it might work for you.
- That sounds interesting and I don't think I would do that because...
- I don't think I would like that but if it feels right to you...

Who knows what is good or bad?

Talking about judging what's best reminds me of the wonderful story in Steve Hagen's book *Buddhism plain and simple* about the

Chinese farmer whose horse runs away. "When his neighbor came to console him the farmer said, 'Who knows what's good or bad?'

When his horse returned the next day with a herd of horses following her, the foolish neighbor came to congratulate him on his good fortune.

'Who knows what's good or bad?' said the farmer.

Then, when the farmer's son broke his leg trying to ride one of the new horses, the foolish neighbor came to console him again.

'Who knows what's good or bad?' said the farmer.

When the army passed through, conscripting men for the war, they passed over the farmer's son because of his broken leg. When the foolish man came to congratulate the farmer that his son would be spared, again the farmer said, 'Who knows what's good or bad?"

And so on!

Teaching your truth

In my experience, parents are teaching their children their truths all the time. This is just the way of it and it happens automatically. There is no stopping this or interfering with it or lessening it. You can't say one thing and do another and expect your children to listen to your words and not see your actions, because children see. They see you and your behavior and that is the lesson of life you are giving them all the time. Nothing else is possible in the parent-child interaction. That's the reality of it.

My best advice – treat your children as your best friends. As they grow, listen to them. Want for them what they want. Help them realize their dreams. Lock them up and they'll run away, set them free and they might stay close.

**Treat your children as your best friends.
Want for them what they want.**

Your wisdom comes to you as the gift of life itself. And this is life in all its kindness because wisdom, if you think about it, is always kind. Wisdom, if you think about it, is always the gentle way. Wisdom, if you think about it, always sets people free. That is why we call it wisdom!

And that is why when you stay at home with yourself – and mind your own business – your wisdom will draw all things to you. Overextend yourself and you will fall (fail). Stay at home and the whole world comes to you. That too is the way of it.

You could say that the gift of sanity is knowing this. Knowing who you are and what life is – and staying in your own business.

Ode to staying home

So go wherever you want, but stay at home with yourself. Be whomever you want, but stay at home with yourself. Try whatever you want, but stay at home with yourself.

There is an ease to this, a simplicity, which it has taken me a lifetime to discover, learn and experience. There is a magic here that is beyond understanding, a sweetness that is beyond explaining. Stay at home with yourself and perhaps like me, you will find this magic and be comfortable with life, perhaps for the first time in your life.

This is the sweetness of it. Call it being your own best friend. Call it being there for you. Call it minding your own business. Call it peace. But whatever you call it, when you do this, everyone becomes your friend, including you.

No. 6

Follow your passion and
accept the consequences

> **The number 6 cause of suffering and unhappiness is
> not doing what you want
> because you think people will disapprove.**

Why is it we don't do what we want? Why is it we do not follow our passion but instead allow ourselves to get sidetracked into doing all kinds of things that we know in our heart of hearts we don't really want to do?

Is it money, pride or ego that is preventing us from following our dreams? Or it is simply our fear of the disapproval of others? For some it might be that they don't know what their heart's desire is so they just move along or drift with the flow of life, which of course is perfectly OK. But that isn't really what I want to investigate in this chapter. Rather I would like to explore why many of us may find it difficult to honor our deepest passion and heart's desire.

So if you know your heart's desire and are not honoring it, the question is why is this happening? And why do I bring this up in a book about living a happy life? I bring it up because in my experience, a happy, fulfilled life is one that honors our deepest passion and the most profound longings of our hearts. Regrets for roads not taken simply do not make for a happy life.

If any of this rings a bell, then it might be a good idea to explore this question more fully and deepen your internal dialogue with your self, especially if you feel you are off course in terms of living your dreams! In this connection, it might be interesting to start by asking yourself how and when you discovered you were not fully honoring yourself? What was the trigger? Did something dramatic happen or did you just wake up one morning and realize that you were making poor choices and not honoring the deepest longings of your heart? Did you have an utterly clear moment when you saw your choices and how the momentum of your life was moving you in directions that were not honoring who you really are? And that you were allowing this to happen against your better judgment? What brought on this realization? Was it a close call with death? A sudden illness or change of fortune? The loss of a loved one? The end of a relationship? The loss of a job? Moving to a new place? Or was it just because you felt it was time to look at your life and take stock? And as a result, you found yourself sitting in a chair, gazing out of the window, with the bitter taste of regret in your mouth?

Obviously if this has happened to you, it was probably not a pleasant discovery. But as far as I can see, it's better to wake up sooner than later. Everything I write about in this book is about living a more conscious life. And seeing the reality of our situation is always a good place to start. This is because seeing what is and being honest with ourselves about what we see can help us make better decisions and choices in the now present moment.

Survival and financial pressure

When we are in conflict when it comes to following our passion in life – be it choosing an education, a job, a career, a partnership, or a path in life – there can be many reasons. The first and most obvious is the question of survival and making money. So you may be thinking that most of us can't just run off and follow our dreams; we have to make a living! Most of us have responsibilities like families to support and children to take care of. But still there can be dilemmas. Here are some examples of what I'm talking about.

The young career executive and family man

Michael is a hard-working man in his mid-thirties. He's very bright and talented. Right now he has a well-paid job at a big corporation and his prospects of making a career in the industry are very good. He can easily advance along this pathway and become a top executive if he wants. He's married and his wife is expecting their second child. They are very happy and they just bought a bigger house in a nicer area. Now the thing is, this man's passion is music. He loves music, likes to go to concerts, buys all the latest releases, knows a lot about the industry, and his dream is to become a music producer. But he has no contacts or job opportunities that can take him in the direction he wants to go at the moment. What should he do? He can't just drop his job at the company where he works because he's got responsibilities. He has a new house to pay for and another child on the way. Of course no one forced him to do any of this. He bought the new house and wants to support his family because that's his idea of the good life. But what about his dream of becoming a music producer? How can he meet his obligations and honor his dream at the same time? Because of these conflicting interests and desires, he sometimes feels trapped. He can't just throw his present career away and pursue his dream. Or can he?

The working mother turned healer

Sonja is in her mid-forties and has been working for the government for the past 20 years. Her comfortable office job is well paid and she has security and a good pension plan. Her two children are in their late teens and her husband is an engineer. They live in a nice house in the suburbs and they are saving up to buy a summerhouse. Over the last couple of years, Sonja has become more and more interested in alternative healing and has been going to courses and lectures about the healing arts. She also started practicing yoga and eating more healthy foods. Recently she discovered she has a talent for healing massage and now wants to start practicing what she has learned. Should she quit her good government job and open her own massage clinic? What if her husband doesn't think it's a good idea? How will it affect her family's financial situation and their plans to buy a summerhouse? What will her friends and family say? Is it possible for Sonja to follow her dream and still meet her commitments? Because of these conflicting interests and desires, she sometimes feels trapped. She can't just throw away her present career and pursue her dream. Or can she?

In situations like this, how can we become more conscious? How can we better understand the mechanisms behind our apparently conflicting interests?

Do we have a choice?

First of all, do we have a choice?

When we analyze what we do in situations like the ones described above, one of the first things that springs to mind is this: It is often a question of lifestyle and values. And our lifestyle and values depend on so many things – the society we live in, our culture, our background, our education and our religion just to mention a few.

The next obvious thing that springs to mind is that it's a question of priorities. We are always weighing our options because whether we are really conscious about what we are doing or not, we all know that everything has a price and that there are no free lunches!

So you might want to ponder on the following:

1. Is there a conflict between your culture, your background, your religion, your family's expectations and your dreams? For many, the answer may be yes. And if this is the case, what are your options? In other words, what is the cost of making choices that your culture, religion or family may disapprove of? Obviously there will be a big

difference, for example, between the situation and options of women in Afghanistan and the situation and options of women in Scandinavia.

2. Is it a question of basic survival? Is there a conflict between your passion and your basic survival? For many in the West, the answer is probably no. This is because for most people in the West, basic survival is not the issue. Most of us have a roof over our heads and food on our table. So we are more concerned with living happy, fulfilled lives.

3. Do we need material comfort to live a happy, fulfilled life? This too is a complex issue and the answer to this question will of course vary from person to person and from culture to culture. For some people, material comfort is the ultimate good and for others it can be less important, but it is in the nature of life here on earth that some level of material possessions is required for our survival. But obviously our feelings about the level of material comfort we believe we require to live a good life can have a strong influence on our choices and on our ability to pursue our heart's desire. Especially when following one's heart's desire does not seem to be a moneymaking proposition!

The questions above are all more general and cultural and are always good to contemplate in our attempt to live a more conscious and fulfilled life. But in this particular chapter I'd also like to take a closer look at some of the more personal aspects of following your passion.

Becoming more conscious

My basic premise in writing this book is that the more conscious we become of the way our minds work and the nature of reality, the better our chances are of living a happy life. So to become more conscious in this area of our lives, it can help to ask the following questions and answer them as specifically as possible:

1. What do I want?
2. What do I have to do to get what I want?
    a) What is the cost of getting what I want?
    b) Is it worth it? (Is getting what I want worth the cost?)
    c) Realize there are no "free lunches". Everything in life has a price. (This is another way of saying there is a law of cause and effect.)
3. What do I believe I 'should' do?
    a) Is there a conflict between what I want to do and what I believe I should do?
    b) And if there is, what are the conflicting beliefs? And are they true? In other words, what is reality? And what is my story?

Let's take a simple example and try out some of the above questions: Charlotte is 27 and she wants to be a doctor. She started going to medical school when she was 23. She studied and partied and passed several exams and failed some too. When she failed two exams in a row, she began to doubt herself and dropped out of medical school and tried doing other things. But during the next year, she discovered that she couldn't forget her dream of becoming a doctor. Becoming a doctor is truly her passion. Charlotte *wants* to be a doctor! That's just the way it is. And now she's back at medical school and doing very well because she is now clear about what it will cost to become a doctor. She's become realistic. She sees the reality, which is if she wants to become a doctor she has to go to medical school for about 8-10 years, study really hard, and pass all her exams. There is no other way Charlotte can become a doctor. And this means she will have to give up a lot of other things. For one, she cannot go partying as much as she likes or get involved in all kinds of other activities even if she wants to. If Charlotte wants to be a doctor, she has to pay what it costs to get what she wants.

This is a rather straightforward example so far. A simple question of what do I want and am I willing to do what it takes to get what I want.

But what if Charlotte is really going to medical school because she thinks she 'should' go and not because it's her true passion? What if she is going because she knows it will make her mother and father happy? What if her real passion is something completely different, like becoming a professional dancer? If this is the case it may be more difficult for Charlotte to follow her real passion because her family would probably frown upon such a career choice. Charlotte's father is a doctor and she comes from a family of professionals. She has been groomed all her life to get a good education and become a professional of some kind.

If Charlotte is going to medical school because of family pressure, it is probably because she has some underlying beliefs that are preventing her from following her true passion. For example, she may have the underlying belief that what she does can influence other people. In other words she might believe that she can make someone else happy or unhappy (in this case her mother and father). Or she may fear disapproval and the loss of her parents' love because she may have the underlying belief that her parents will only love her if she does what they want her to do. So let's examine these two underlying beliefs for a moment:

Underlying belief: I am responsible for the happiness of others.
Charlotte may be thinking: If I don't go to medical school it will make my mother and father unhappy. Here it could be a good idea for Charlotte to ask herself: Is this true? Will her mother and father be unhappy if Charlotte doesn't go to medical school? And if the answer to this is yes, the next question is who is responsible for making Charlotte's mother and father happy. Is Charlotte responsible for her mother and father's happiness? Is their

happiness Charlotte's job or is it Charlotte's mother and father's job? Another relevant question for Charlotte if she is worried about her parent's unhappiness is whose business is Charlotte minding?

Underlying belief: My parents won't love me if they disapprove of what I do. Or *my parents won't love me if I do what I want.*
Charlotte might also be thinking: If I don't go to medical school, my mother and father will be disappointed in me and they won't love me anymore. Here it is a good idea to ask: Is this true? Will Charlotte's parents really stop loving her if she doesn't go to medical school? The question here is – is the love that Charlotte's parents feel for Charlotte based on her career choices or can it survive a decision they don't like? Another important question here is what does loving someone have to do with their career choices? Is there any connection between love and people agreeing with each other?

It took me many, many years to discover that loving someone and agreeing with them are two different things. I had the mistaken underlying belief that if you love someone, you will agree with them. This insane belief brought me so much anguish because it makes it very difficult to love anyone! And it brings so much pain because it leaves you thinking how can I love this person since I don't agree with him/her about anything at all! When I began waking up to reality without my stories, I discovered that people just don't agree with each other and that this has nothing to do with loving them! Now I can relax because I love lots of people I don't agree with. In fact, everyone I love disagrees with me! This discovery has been such a great relief for me. Now I can see that love is our nature – which has very little to do with our minds and our stories and our opinions. We just love. And that's it!

Who is manipulating you?

But to go back to Charlotte and the questions. When you start asking yourself these kinds of questions at first you may well come to the conclusion that you are being manipulated by other people. But is this true? In my experience I have found that you can only be manipulated by what other people say you should or should not do (or by what other people expect of you), if you believe their 'shoulds'. By this I mean they can only manipulate you if you agree with and accept their 'shoulds' because you think they are correct. This means you share the same belief system and 'shoulds' as the people you think are manipulating you. So you need to question your beliefs because the question is still who is really manipulating you? Is it someone else or are you being manipulated by your own uninvestigated beliefs? If you want to be free, find out what you really believe. Question the beliefs you have that make you suffer. Find out if they are true. Find out what you believe in relation to what other people tell you and believe. Do you agree with their stories? And if so, why? Are these stories supporting you and helping you live a happy life or are they causing you stress and making you suffer.

Good questions to ask are:

- What is true for you? Not what other people say, but what you say. No one else can say or has the right to say what's true for you.
- What is good for you? Again not what other people say is good for you (no matter how well meaning). No one else can say or has the right to say what is good for you.
- What should your life path be? Again no one else can say or has the right to say what your life path should be.
- What do you feel? How can anyone else know? And if they say they do, they are only guessing or projecting their own feelings on you. No one else can say or has the right to say what you should feel.

There are no easy explanations as to why you are you or why you feel the way you do. You just do. Nor are there any easy explanations when it comes to explaining why you are the way you are. That's just the way it is. Another common uninvestigated belief is that *we should be able to explain (or justify) the way we are*. But the reality is that we can't. And who says that we need to justify or explain why we are like we are? Where is it written that this is a condition of life? If you believe that you are supposed to justify yourself, you are setting yourself up for pain and anguish because how can you do this? How can you satisfy anyone – when you can't even explain you to yourself!

So if you believe that you 'should' be able to explain or justify why you passionately want to be a music producer or a healer or a doctor, you open yourself to all kinds of manipulation. But if you really 'see', you will discover that in the final analysis no one can really explain why they are like they are. Why does Charlotte want to be a doctor, really? Why does Michael want to be a music producer and Sonja a healer? You can come up with a million and one possible explanations but the truth is you can never know exactly why we are like we are. But we are! And that's reality.

The way of it

The reality is also that we all know when we are following our passion or our heart's desire because it feels right. Everyone has experienced this feeling of 'rightness' at some time in his/her life. It's called integrity. And it's easy to recognize. It's a sense of real comfort. A feeling that life is good and that life is moving freely in and through you. It's that feeling of ease, when you experience no discomfort, no obstructions, no limitations, no doubts. You know it's good because it's the free flow of life through you, as if the whole universe is working in and through you. And in truth, this is what is happening. This is the reality of it. Because when you are in the flow, everything in life *is* working in and through you and with you. And that's what makes it feel so right.

So we discover that what all our arbitrary beliefs and belief systems really do is block the free, spontaneous expression of life in and through us. And this is why we suffer. This is why we feel discomfort. This is why we experience what we call a conflict of interests. Something is blocking the free flow of life in and through us. Something is limiting our freedom. Something is preventing us from expressing the will and creativity of the universe. And this makes us suffer. This is what suffering is. Limitation.

When we understand this, we understand that what we call our true desire, our heart's desire, is really our becoming conscious of this free flowing life that is working in and through us. Or you could say we become aware that our heart's desire is actually the will of the entire universe or of the great universal creativity expressing itself through us.

The pain of not listening

What happens when we don't listen? When we don't follow the inner voice and listen to our heart's desire. When we do what other people want us to do or what they say we should do or when we follow our uninvestigated beliefs and 'shoulds'? I can only speak for myself and tell you that in my experience, trying to live up to my own uninvestigated 'shoulds' and beliefs has caused me so much unnecessary anguish. It's easy to say this now when I am able to see what I was doing so much more clearly, but when I was in the midst of it, all I can say is that it was truly hell! I guess that is what hell is – unconsciously causing ourselves so much pain and suffering! Until we wake up and discover that this is the only suffering there is. The pain and suffering we cause ourselves.

**The only suffering there is,
is the suffering we cause ourselves.**

My deathbed technique

Many years ago when I began contemplating the challenge of following my inner impulses and my heart's desire, I developed what I called "my deathbed technique". I found that the deathbed technique is a great exercise when I'm feeling insecure, weak or shaky and uncertain about following my heart's desire, especially when I fear the disapproval of others. The exercise is a kind of creative visualization technique in which I imagine myself on my deathbed, looking back at this moment where I lack the courage of my convictions! And then I try to envision how I will feel on my deathbed if I do not honor the highest and best in myself at this very moment in time. For me, it's always a devastating thought and makes decision-making a lot easier!

The technique helps me envision how I will feel if I do not take the road which can lead me up higher and closer to being fully aligned with who I am.

When playing around with this technique, I also discovered that you can use it to strengthen your resolve in the little, everyday situations of life that also demand courage. Take an ordinary situation like this: You are a woman sitting in a café with your girlfriend drinking a cappuccino. At the next table, there are some interesting men and you'd really like to talk to them. Your shyness, your fear of disapproval, your ideas about what women 'should' and 'shouldn't' do, and your fear of making a fool of yourself prevent you from turning to them and saying something. If you remember the deathbed technique at a moment like this, it can really help. You can ask yourself how you will feel when you are 92 and leaving this planet if you look back at this moment of your life? How will it feel to realize that you had the gift of life but didn't dare to follow your impulse to talk to the men (who are just human beings like you) at the next table because you were afraid of disapproval? Because you were afraid of doing something that would take you out of your comfort zone. You will probably discover that you will feel rather ridiculous when you view this situation from the larger perspective of your life. And from the larger perspective, what is the worse that can happen if you follow your inner impulse and step out of your comfort zone? The men at the next table might ignore you? They might laugh at you? They might think you are dumb or not be interested in talking to you and your girlfriend? And if that happens, so what? Not following your inner impulses in all the little situations like this in life also means you miss so many great opportunities to meet new people, have fun, make new contacts, and widen your circle of friends. You can never know where following your heart's desire can lead. But being inhibited or limited by your concepts will most certainly prevent you from acting spontaneously and prevent you from finding out! So in situations like this, the deathbed technique is the perfect tool to show you how limiting your concepts may be when it comes to living a happy, fulfilled and exciting life!

Do the right thing and accept the consequences

> **The number 7 cause of suffering and unhappiness is
> not doing the right thing
> because you're afraid of the consequences.**

In the early 1960s when I was 18, the Vietnam War was really starting to turn ugly. My boyfriend Steve had just dropped out of college and was immediately drafted into the army. Steve and I were against the Vietnam War. My father was a military man and worked at the Pentagon, so our opposition to the war wasn't very popular in my family. At that time, there was the draft in the United States so Steve had only two options – join the army or go to jail for five years. He had no chance of becoming a conscientious objector because at that time you could only get conscientious objector status on religious grounds and Steve definitely wasn't religious. The protest movement hadn't really begun yet in the United States and Steve and I felt very alone with our choices. But it was a question of doing the right thing and we had only our lives and our bodies to do it with – so we did. We decided we would not be a part of a war that we thought was unjust. So I ran away from home and Steve ran from the army – and together we went underground. We left the United States and after two years on the run and many adventures, we ended up getting political asylum in Sweden, a country that opposed American involvement in Vietnam.

Doing the right thing

Because of this experience, I learned at an early age that doing the right thing isn't always easy and that all one's choices always have consequences – both for oneself and for the world. In the case of the Vietnam War, fortunately there were many other young Americans who felt the same way as Steve and I did and eventually America withdrew from Vietnam, but only after so many lives were tragically destroyed.

For me personally, this decision changed the course of my whole life and resulted in me leaving the country of my birth at a very young age and building a new life in Scandinavia where I still live today. Many years later when I saw my father for the last time, he cried and apologized for not understanding or supporting me way back then when I was young. Such is the way of it.

The impulse to do the right thing burns brightly in each of us.

It is our nature, the heart of us, which is love. When we oppose our innermost nature, we suffer and so do others. That is why I feel so strongly that if you want to live a happy life, do not cover up this urge, this flame, this bright impulse to do the right thing (which is always an expression of love) – regardless of the cost. This flame is your morning star, this flame is your guiding light, this flame is the heart of you.

Doing the right thing on a daily basis

Doing the right thing is not just a social-political activity or just about doing the right thing in the big areas of your life; it's also a daily activity because every moment of our lives we are faced with choices big and small. And every choice, every action has consequences. This is because of the law of cause and effect, which is always in operation and which means that every thought, word and action sets in motion a chain of events and happenings that echo down through the ages. We live in a universe of interdependence where no man or woman is an island, but where each one of us is part of the same fabric, part of the same web of life, each inextricably influencing each other and the whole.

That is why it is so important to be mindful and pay attention to what we are thinking, saying and doing. Because everything we think, say and do has consequences. When we are mindful and always try to align ourselves with our true inner knowingness, we are living and acting with as much awareness as we are capable of – in both the public and private arena. More than this we cannot do.

With this growing awareness, we discover that no matter where we are or who we are, we are always being given the opportunity to do the right thing. Regardless of our station in life, regardless of our culture, age or sex, choices are appearing before us all the time, each and every day. This is the way of it as it unfolds before us. Events may be big or small, but all events and activities are equally worthy of our attention. Every event, every issue, every situation is awaiting our stamp – your stamp and mine – the stamp of our integrity – the stamp that expresses our highest vision of what life can be on earth.

In every case, in every situation, it is our intention that counts. Intention is the golden key and determines our focus. We must ask ourselves: Is our intention for the highest Good? Is our intention for peace, love and harmony? Is our intention to avoid or end suffering? These are the questions we need to ask ourselves over and over again as we proceed through our day. These are the questions we need to ask as we reflect on our choices and our activities.

Our values

In order to do the right thing, it helps to clarify our values. What do we believe in – you and I? Ask yourself what do you stand for? If you don't know the answer to these questions, find out. Because without knowing what you stand for, you lack a compass and it will be difficult to act clearly and consistently. So find out what you believe in. Find out what's important to you.

Where do you draw the line? Where are your limits?

Do you believe in freedom? I, for one, do. I am passionate about being free. Free to be and do as I please. Free to be myself – and freedom for everyone else to be themselves too. For me freedom means many things. Freedom of opportunity. Freedom for women. Freedom of religion. Freedom to come and go as you please. Freedom to choose the profession of your choice. Freedom from fear and hunger. Freedom to pursue the life of your dreams. Freedom regardless of your race or color. Freedom to think as you please. Freedom to be the unique individual that you are. And with this goes a deep respect for the freedom of others.

If you believe in the importance of freedom as I do, then we have to explore what we mean specifically by this concept we call freedom. And then we have to ask ourselves – what am I doing to encourage the precious freedom I believe in and value so highly? Where in my life am I not standing up for the freedom I believe in? Where am I letting freedom down? Where am I not setting other people free – both in practice and in my own mind? How am I limiting others and not setting them free? If, for example, I am minding other people's business, am I setting them free? If I am minding their business it means I am not trusting in their integrity and intelligence to serve them well in the same way that I expect my own integrity and intelligence to serve me well. Am I generalizing about the races or the sexes and thus not setting people free? Am I generalizing about people's ages and thus not setting them free? Where am I failing freedom? Where am I not setting myself free? If I believe in freedom, I must practice freedom and be the freedom I believe in.

The same goes for all the other things we value so highly.

Do you value generosity – then practice generosity and become the generous person you believe everyone should be. Find out where you are not being generous and living up to this value in your life and make it your project to become the generous person you want to meet in the world. Do you believe in loving-kindness? Then practice loving-kindness and find out where in your life you are failing to be loving and kind and become the loving-kindness you want to see in the world. Are you against violence? Then find out where in your life you are being violent. Are your thoughts and words about yourself or others violent? If so it's time to begin practicing non-violence in your own mind first – and then in your close personal relationships. If you believe in non-violence, make sure you are non-violent in all your thoughts, words and activities. In other words, be and live the change you want to see in the world.

> **"Be the change you want to see in the world." Gandhi**

Afraid of the consequences?

If you are not honoring what you feel 'doing the right thing' is in some area of your life, it is probably because you are afraid of the consequences. In our everyday life, the consequences can be less dramatic than in the political arena, but they can still be devastating. The consequences of doing what we believe is right in our daily lives can include the loss of money, difficulty in surviving, being ostracized, being scorned, being ridiculed, just to name a few. Here are some examples of what I mean:

Leaving your marriage. You are desperately unhappy in your marriage but are afraid of leaving your husband because it means you will be a single mother with two small children. If you leave your husband, you will be a lot poorer. In fact you will be quite poor. That will be the consequence. So it will be more difficult to survive. What do you do?

Saying no to a well-paid job. You are offered a good job at a cigarette company. It is well paid and a great career opportunity for you. But you feel that smoking is dangerous to people's health so it would be wrong to work for a company that endangers people's lives. But if you say no to the job, you fear that the recruitment agency that is helping you will not be interested in finding another good job opportunity for you. What do you do?

Saying no to an assignment. You have your own graphic design firm and get offered a great assignment from a company you worked for previously. The last time you worked for this company, you discovered that they were involved in unethical business practices. You don't want to work for a company like this, but saying no means passing up a nice chunk of money, money that your company could really use at the moment. What do you do?

Standing up for someone. You are out with your friends and they start making fun of someone or mobbing someone (either present or absent) because of their race or religion. You feel uncomfortable and know the right thing to do would be to stand up for this person and tell the others to stop behaving like this. But doing so will probably make your friends ostracize you or scorn you. What do you do?

Buying power. In general, we have a lot of power as consumers. How do we use this power on a daily basis? For example, are you buying products that you know pollute the environment – or products that you know are made using child labor – or products that come from companies with unethical business practices? Where do we put our money? This is a very important question. Do you think about what you buy and support with your choices as a consumer? Again, every time we buy something, each one of us has the opportunity to influence the world situation and practice doing what we consider the right thing.

Who sets the standards?

Apropos doing the right thing, who sets the standards for right and wrong anyway? This is a difficult and complex question that we all face. When we begin to look deeply into the matter, we discover it is extremely difficult to set down any hard and fast rules about right and wrong because each situation is different and unique in its own special way. Each situation requires us to be fully present and carefully scrutinize what is going on. But still, we all ask ourselves, is there a way to judge, is there a way to know what to do in each situation? Is there a compass? And if so, where can it be found?

In my own experience, I have found that by being present and honest – and by standing quietly and firmly in my own integrity, I am able to get in touch with my own inner wisdom. And this wisdom is always an impulse for the good, for love, an impulse for freedom, an impulse to help and comfort and find a way out of suffering – for myself and for others. I believe this fundamental urge can be found everywhere, in everyone, and that basically it is an urge toward the good in life. It's like stardust and it's in our cells, always calling us. And when we are quiet and listen, we can hear the voice of our inner wisdom speaking. Then we know when we are in sync with the goodness that is our nature.

> **The impulse to the good is like stardust, it's in our cells.**

Good questions to ask yourself

If you feel you are having difficult getting in touch with your inner wisdom and feel unsure about what to do in a given situation, you can ask yourself the following questions to prompt your own inner knowingness to show its face:

- How would I want others to treat me in this situation?
- What is my intention in this situation?
- Am I only thinking of myself and my own benefit – or am I taking into consideration how this situation will affect the other people who are involved?
- How will my thoughts, words and actions affect the situation and the other people?
- Will my choices and actions help avoid or ease suffering?
- Do I have any idea what the long-term consequences of my thoughts, words and actions could or will be? Have I thought about this? Can I envision some of the possible consequences? In other words, what will this activity lead to?

Questions like these can help us clarify our intention and become aware of the consequences of various courses of action. The more light we can cast upon our thinking, judgments and activities, the easier it becomes to act in accordance with our deepest inner wisdom.

Universal standards

There are of course certain universal standards. Among these, there is, for example, the Golden Rule of Jesus. Ages ago he said "Do unto others as you would have them do unto you." This is like asking the first question listed above – how would we like others to treat us in this situation? In other words, what would we want someone else to do to us if the tables were turned? How would we want someone else to treat us? How would we like someone else to act towards us? This can often help us know what to do because we all know that we don't want to suffer. We know, for example, we wouldn't want anyone to drop a bomb on our home or kill our family – or steal our money – or insult our beliefs – or take away our freedom. So why would we want to do anything that would make someone else suffer these very same things?

Jesus also said, "Let he who is without sin cast the first stone." Again, being critical and judgmental is not a great idea either. Better to get our own houses in order first. In other words, let us be the change we want to see in the world first.

Buddhist philosophy teaches another excellent and practical approach which we can call 'non-doing'. Instead of doing towards others, the Buddha-dharma teaches us never do anything that will harm another. In other words to refrain from doing what we don't want other people to do to us! This translates into refraining from harmful thoughts, words and actions. In the Dhammapada, the Buddha said, "Do no harm, act for the good, purify the mind." This is the Buddhist concept of harmlessness, which is an excellent compass for living in a world of turmoil and constant change. Holding our actions up against this concept can help us become mindful of the consequences of our actions and help us live more responsibly.

As far as I understand it, interwoven into the concept of harmlessness, the Buddhists believe in the importance of being 'awake'. When we are 'awake' and can 'see' reality for what it is – doing the right thing (which they call right action) is natural and spontaneous. This is because when you are awake, you can see what the consequences of your behavior might be and will thus avoid doing harm. You will naturally not want to say or do anything that leads to confusion and suffering. Since the Buddhists also believe in karma, i.e., that all our actions have consequences, they point out that our intention or motivation is the most important factor. When our intention or motivation is to be 'awake' and end the suffering of others, we set in motion an event line, which supports the good of others.

When you 'see', you can also see what causes suffering.

The common thread

In general, when we explore the world's great spiritual teachings, we find a common thread running through them all and that thread is universal love and the oneness of all humankind. Without understanding our interconnectedness, without understanding that we are all part of this thing we call life, it is obviously very difficult to know what to think, how to judge, and how to do the right thing on a daily basis. But when we 'see' that we are all part and parcel of the same cloth, it becomes much easier to know what is right and appropriate in every now moment.

Finding the Gandhi within

Gandhi is one of my greatest heroes. I admire him so much because he continually tried to practice what he considered 'doing the right thing' and live the oneness of humankind in his daily life. Because of his ruthless honesty, earnestness, intention to relieve suffering, and enormous dedication, he changed the course of history. When we read about his life, we find that he was constantly experimenting and trying to do the right thing (as the title of his autobiography so eloquently expresses it *The Story of My Experiments with Truth*) – and we also discover that he was willing to accept the consequences of his actions. His practice of ahimsa (non-violence) and non-violent civil disobedience was based on the realization that it could cost him his life and he said more than once, "I am prepared to die, but there is no cause for which I am prepared to kill." (See *Gandhi* the film by Richard Attenborough from 1982 for an inspiring look at Gandhi's life and philosophy.)

According to his biographers, Gandhi's spiritual reference book was the *Bhagavad Gita* and the end of Chapter Two summed up Gandhi's life philosophy. According to historians, he meditated on this verse every single day of his life. I quote it here for your inspiration:

From the *Bhagavad Gita*, Chapter 2: The Illumined Man:

"Sri Krishna says:
They live in wisdom
Who see themselves in all and all in them,
Whose love for the Lord of Love has consumed
Every selfish desire and sense craving
Tormenting the heart. Not agitated
By grief nor hankering after pleasure,
They live free from lust and fear and anger.
Fettered no more by selfish attachments,
They are not elated by good fortune
Nor depressed by bad. Such are the seers...

When you keep thinking about sense objects,
Attachment comes. Attachment breeds desire,
The lust of possession, which when thwarted,
Burns to anger. Anger clouds the judgment
And robs you of the power to learn from past
Mistakes. Lost is the discriminative
Faculty, and your life is utter waste.

But when you move amidst the world of sense,
From attachment and aversion freed,
There comes the peace in which all sorrow ends,
And you live in the wisdom of the Self.

The disunited mind is far from wise;
How can it meditate? How be at peace?
When you know no peace, how can you know joy?
When you let your mind follow the siren
Call of the senses, they carry away
Your better judgment as a cyclone drives
A boat off the charted course to its doom...

They are forever free who have broken
Out of the ego-cage of *I* and *mine*
To be united with the Lord of Love.
This is the supreme state. Attain thou this
And pass from death to immortality."

From the book, *Gandhi The Man – The Story of His Transformation* by Eknath Easwaran.

Living change, being peace

For me I feel the most important thing I can do is be the change I want to see in the world. And this goes for all areas of my life – in my personal relationships with my family and friends and in all my social, political and business dealings. I believe that if I want to see peace in the world, I must be that peace first. For me this means first of all ending the war inside my own mind and then secondly finding and being peace in my closest relationships – with my family and friends – and then in my community and in my world. This is the only peace I can be, know or experience. No other peace is possible for me.

So all I can do is ask myself, where am I failing to be the peace I want to see in the world? Where am I not being peace? Where am I in conflict? What are my intentions in every situation? Are they peaceful? And how will my actions affect each situation? Am I being the change I want to see in the world? Am I being peace?

A word about generalizations

In connection with the above, I think this is a good place to talk about generalizations. Why? Because in my experience, generalizations often are blocking the peace we so much want and preventing us from seeing the truth about the individuals and situations we are dealing with in this now moment. If we want peace between individuals, groups, and nations, then it's vital that we cast the light of awareness on generalizations and see how we unconsciously use them to blind ourselves to the reality that is unfolding right in front of our eyes.

But let's define generalization first. By generalization I mean a statement that matches a certain category or group of people to a certain type of behavior. Webster's dictionary says generalization is: "a proposition asserting something to be true of all members of a certain class..." Generalization is a kind of "black and white" thinking because we are making everything so extreme, so "either/or". And reality is not like that – reality is more in between, more nuanced. In its most offensive and dangerous form, generalization is blatant, negative cultural stereotyping that is based on insufficient facts.

Be honest with yourself

When talking about generalizations, I believe it's important that we are honest with ourselves and by this I mean bringing the issue of generalizations home to ourselves. If we want to eliminate the malice spread by generalizations, we must look at what we are doing in our own lives. So I suggest you ask yourself most specifically – how often do you generalize? (Are you even aware of the fact that you might be generalizing?) How often do you judge the person before you – without really knowing anything about this person – by his/her sex, age, appearance, ethnic background, and clothes/profession, and social class?

In my experience, most of us are generalizing quite unconsciously a lot of the time. For example, we meet someone and we see by the way he is dressed that he's a businessman – and right away all our stories about businessmen kick in. For someone who is striving to make it in the world of business, the response could be the greatest respect and a sense of awe for the man standing there. For someone else who is campaigning against social injustice in the poorest nations of Africa, it could be a sense of disapproval and contempt. And both responses probably arise without the person knowing anything specific about this particular man. It's just a conditioned response based on general-izations (which are based on our beliefs and stories) about businessmen. The reality could be that this businessman is the head of a company that's working to bring low-cost irrigation equipment to poor farmers in southern Africa. The reality could be that this businessman has found a way to funnel money from one of his company's most profitable projects into his own pocket. Who knows? The point is when you catch yourself doing this, put your stories and generalizations on hold and decide to deal with the man in front of you. Wait until you find out who he is and what he stands for before you decide how to deal with this person. Give yourself time to find out what's true about this person without generalizing or stereotyping people by their class, sex, ethnic background, etc. Give yourself – and the other person – a chance! This is doing the right thing.

Dealing with generalizations

In addition to becoming mindful of when you are generalizing yourself, how do you deal with generalizations coming from other people you meet during the course of your day? Obviously the first and most important step is just to become aware of what a generalization is. When we understand what a generalization is and how dangerous it can be to our ability to get along with each other, it is easy to recognize a generalization when it pops up in conversations with other people. When this happens, instead of letting it pass, the best thing you can do is to question the validity of the statement you are being presented with.

When, for example, a man says to you that all women are lousy drivers, you could ask: Is it true that all women are lousy drivers? Where's the proof? You can say well my friend Martha is an excellent driver and she's a woman – and so is my friend Maria. You can say in fact I know quite a few women who are good drivers. And you can ask, what about men? You could say I can think of quite a few men who are not such good drivers! And so on. Rather than just letting a blatant generalization slide by, stand up and question it. You don't have to be confrontational when doing this, just keep your focus and examine the statement. All you are really doing is simply asking: Is it true? Why is this true? Are you sure it's true? Where's the proof?

Instead of generalizing, you can ask the other person to substitute a more accurate and qualified statement instead of generalizing. You can suggest or use statements like… 'As far as I know'… or 'it seems to me'… or 'in my experience'. These modifications help us own what we are saying and take responsibility for our words.

The bottom line is that generalizations separate us from each other instead of helping us recognize our oneness.

Generalizations separate us.
Love brings us together.

The intention of oneness

If you believe, as I do, in the essential oneness of all life then you will understand the importance of our belief and intention of oneness. When our intention is to support the oneness of all life, it will guide all our thoughts, words and actions. When this happens, our natural urge is to move to relieve suffering wherever we meet it. We don't want to suffer nor do we want anyone else in our family to suffer, it's as simple as that. And since everyone is a member of our family, this urge includes everyone. Looking at our words and actions from this perspective, we know that anything that relieves suffering, brings us together, and creates harmony is positive, while anything that separates and causes more suffering is negative.

Another vision

Sometimes I ask myself, what would happen to the world if everyone started living more like I do? And by this I mean, what would happen if everyone started pulling back their focus from all the outer distractions that most of us are so engrossed in and began turning their focus inward?

> "Sitting quietly, doing nothing, spring comes
> and the grass grows by itself." Zen proverb

What would happen if more and more people preferred sitting quietly to, for example, going traveling, going shopping, watching television, or going to the movies? What would be the social consequences? It's a fun experiment to ask yourself this question. Because when you begin to contemplate this, what do you get? Think about it – what would our world look like if more people realized they could find the happiness they seek by sitting quietly and turning their focus inward instead of looking to the outer for happiness? Any way you look at it, the consequences – socially, politically, economically – would be mind-boggling. Here are a few things that come to mind, just for starters...

Let's take the travel industry first of all. If people traveled less, the travel industry would slow down drastically and decline. There'd be less air traffic and a lot less traffic on the roads. And without so much air and road traffic, air pollution would immediately decline. We'd also need less oil because we would be consuming less oil so we'd be less dependent on oil and on the Middle East. This would have enormous political (and social) consequences and change the world political scene drastically. And since the world would be burning less fossil fuel for travel, global warming would slow down too. If people traveled less, we wouldn't need to make so many cars and in the long run a lot of people probably wouldn't need cars at all. This would translate into a lot less pressure on the environment in general and on building roads in particular. If there were less travel, we wouldn't need so many airports either. All of this would put less pressure on the planet's beautiful natural resources too. With fewer tourists, there'd be less building going on in all the beautiful and exotic spots around the globe. The beaches would stay cleaner and the seas would too. And without so many people traveling, there'd be less noise so the whole world would become a lot quieter. Interesting isn't it? And these are just a few random consequences of what would happen if we shifted our focus and realized that the happiness we seek is within, instead of constantly looking to the outer world for our happiness.

It makes one think doesn't it? Who knows maybe the best thing you can do to fight pollution is to stay home!

> **Sitting quietly, doing nothing may be the best thing you can do for the world.**

And what about shopping? What would happen if people in our consumer society shopped less? At least here in the West almost everyone I know (including me) has far more than we could ever possibly need to live a good life. But shopping and conspicuous consumption are a way of life for so many of us – and a super form of entertainment and distraction too. But let's ask ourselves, what would happen if we shopped less? What would happen if our focus was not so outer-directed and we realized that material possessions are nice but do not make us happy. Of course you might be saying how naïve Barbara, if people shopped less the whole economy would collapse! But is that true? If we shifted our focus, yes it would change the whole world radically, but who can say that the change wouldn't be for the better? And if we didn't shop so much, what would happen? (We could share our wealth with the rest of the world for one.) And let's face it, shopping, when you don't need anything, is simply a way of passing time. It's a form of distraction and it might be fun and stimulate the economy and production of even more useless stuff, but what good does it do you – or anyone – in the long run? The momentary flash of pleasure as your credit card goes through the machine – and then what? Well it does keep your attention focused on outer things – at least for a while. But how long does the rush last? And when it's over, what then? More work and more shopping? More chasing after something, somewhere out there that will make you happy?

Shopping, like travel, is just one of many ways we distract ourselves in our frantic search for happiness. There are countless other ways, like working, making money, watching television, eating, having sex, working out, going to the movies, you name it. The list is long and includes almost anything and everything except sitting quietly in the present moment right now. And when you look at the general drift of society here in the West, you see that everyone is more or less doing it – running through the loops, running after outer distractions – all because almost everyone honestly thinks that happiness is somewhere out there.

The opposite is true

As far as I can see, all this constant chasing after happiness in the outer does is keep us from having time to sit quietly with ourselves – in the now. And this is very interesting, isn't it, especially when you consider the fact that everything I'm saying and writing about in this book about happiness is the exact opposite of chasing happiness in the outer. Everything I'm saying – and most of what all the wise ones have been saying for centuries – is that real happiness is within. Real happiness is our nature. Real happiness is not something we can attain; it's something we are. And at the same time, when we look around, we see that almost everything everyone is doing is the exact opposite – running away from the very place where this real happiness can be found! Which is right here, inside ourselves. What a laugh! And how sad! To think we have it all right here, within ourselves, and what do we do? We just keep missing it – over and over again!

And because we don't know this, what happens? We continue our frantic search for the happiness that keeps eluding us – and we work and we work and we travel, shop, eat, watch TV, have sex, run after relationships, and accumulate and accumulate some more and we're still miserable. We still feel empty – and no amount of working, traveling, shopping, watching TV or having sex can cure us. The ache is still there. The hunger. The emptiness.

But as long as we continue to believe that the good that we seek is somewhere out there – somewhere beyond us – somewhere just around the corner – somewhere out in the future… somewhere else but here now… of course we'll keep on running… and running…

But this behavior – this constant focus on the outer for happiness – this insatiable urge to consume, be entertained, and travel – also has enormous social, political and economic consequences for the planet. Everyone knows that half the world is living in appalling poverty while the other half consumes far more than we can ever possibly need for a good life. As far as I can see, it is impossible not to arrive at the conclusion that the political and social consequences of following the recommendations I make in this book are enormous. And that changing your focus from being so outer-directed to becoming more inner-directed because you want to live a happy life is also one of the best things you can do to create a better world. Seen in this light, seeking your own happiness is not a selfish pursuit at all. On the contrary, when you look deeply, you find it's probably one of the most altruist things in the world you can do!

No. 8

Deal with what is in front of you and forget the rest

> **The number 8 cause of suffering and unhappiness is shadowboxing with illusions instead of dealing with the reality in front of you.**

Are you relating to what's really happening in front of you? Or are you just relating to an illusion? And by that I mean instead of relating to what's really happening in front of your eyes at this very moment, are you relating to your story or your projection about what the events in front of you might mean? I realize this is a radical question – a very radical question indeed. In fact it's so radical that most of us have a hard time just comprehending the question itself. This is because we've probably never thought about our behavior in this light before. In fact, just thinking about our behavior like this requires a radical shift in consciousness.

Why is this so? It is because of the way we automatically tell ourselves stories – without even realizing it – about the meaning of what is unfolding before our eyes, before we even look at it or into it. And when we do this, it prevents us from really being present in this now moment and 'seeing' what's actually going on. So instead of 'seeing' reality, we just lock into our stories and our conditioned responses and run on automatic. We assume quite unconsciously, and generalize and project meaning onto events that they may or may not have. And this robs us of the freshness of each new, now experience, which is life itself, and the gift of the living present moment.

No wonder life seems stale at times. Because of course it is, especially when we keep repeating our old stories and we aren't even here!

But the real question is: Is it possible to really 'see' and relate to what's actually happening in front of us? I for one believe it is possible to wake up to this now moment. And I base my answer on the fact that I actually have experienced this brilliance – the brilliance of being here in this now moment – for shorter or longer periods of time in my life. So yes, my answer is yes, it is possible to wake up and see. But in my experience, this radical shift in awareness can only arise when it is our intention to be awake in this now moment. Because intention is everything.

> **Relate to the man or woman before you.**
> **Not your story of the past or your story of the future.**

But let's take a closer look at what a radical shift in consciousness like this could mean in our lives...

How would it be and how would you act if you were just relating to the person standing before you instead of acting and relating to your assumptions and stories about this person – all of which are probably pure speculation and illusion? It's pretty hard to imagine isn't it! So let's give it a try.

To make it easy, let's say the person in front of you is your mother. There she is – Mom in all her glory – right! And she's right there, standing in front of you, and amazingly enough, without even saying a single word or doing anything at all, she triggers a whole battery of highly charged emotions in you right? Based on what? Based on a lot of things of course. Based on all the many past experiences you've had with her – and on all the stories you are telling yourself about what all these many past experiences mean – both good and bad. So here you are, standing with this woman – who happens to be Mom in all her glory – and you're either happy to see her, or upset, or sad, or irritated or pissed off... all depending on the stories you are telling yourself about Mom. Right? We've all been there and done that...

But let's stop the movie for a moment and bring ourselves back to reality. Back to this now moment – and drop our stories just for a minute. Then what do we have right now? Well right now we have this woman standing right before us. Keeping the intention to be awake in this now present moment what more do we have? Well we see she's an older woman and she's standing there with her shopping bag. She just walked in the door and looks a bit flustered. What more do you know about her from looking at her in this now moment? Not much else. Maybe she looks tired, maybe she's smiling, maybe she's... If you are awake in this now moment everything will register in your consciousness. But much more than this you cannot possibly know from this now moment. So the question is – and don't laugh but try it – if you didn't know anything about this woman who is your mother who just walked in the door, how would you act? Who would you be without your story about Mom? How would you treat her? I can hear you saying, yeah right, but it's just not possible. But give it a try anyway before you completely dismiss this outrageous idea... just let it simmer in your consciousness for a few moments and see what it brings. Why do I ask you to do this? Because I found it can be very liberating to try shifting our focus like this – even just for a few moments. So please give it a try.

Entering new territory

OK so just put the book down and imagine that you are now meeting your mother without knowing her as you think you do. Imagine meeting her today without the past, without your childhood memories and your stories. What would it be like? What would it feel like? With the knowledge you now have as a grown up person without your so-called past, what would happen? What would happen if you could turn off your story for just a few minutes? How would your interaction with this human being be?

It's pretty hard to imagine, isn't it? And just thinking about it feels like entering completely new territory.

So you are still standing there with this woman who is your mother – minus your story. What do you do now? What would the inner knowingness in you do in the presence of this woman without your story?

First of all you would have to look at her carefully to find out what to do. And in this process, you would naturally and without any effort at all "see" her much more clearly. This would happen automatically because you would have to be present in this now moment to see her and know what to do next. You would have to look at the reality of the woman standing before you otherwise you wouldn't have the slightest clue what to do next. So you would open your eyes and look. You would inhale her.

And what would you discover? That you don't really know her at all? That she's not the woman you thought she was. That she's looking tired? That there is kindness in her voice? That she could probably use a nice cup of tea? That she has a funny way of talking or that she's acting like she just arrived from outer space? Or that she's a drama queen? A complainer? Or that she's violating your boundaries? What would you find if you really looked? What would it be like? Try it with your mother now. Try to envision meeting her and looking at her with no story...

An interesting experience

This is an interesting exercise isn't it, even though you may say it's not possible, especially with our mothers! But it might just be especially true when it comes to our mothers because we have so many stories about them! It's also interesting to notice that when we're really present in a situation we naturally tend to be much more assertive and take better care of ourselves – even with our mothers! So if you're present and your mom starts telling you how to run your life when you didn't ask for her advice, you might find yourself telling her kindly but firmly that you're all grown up now and that she should back off and mind her own business! Wouldn't it be nice to be able to do this without having to go completely ballistic! (See Chapter No. 3 for more about assertiveness and mothers.)

Once this understanding hits home, we can try transferring this powerful insight to the way we interact with the other people we meet on our pathway. When we do this, we discover the same thing, over and over again no matter who we're with. We spend so much of our mental energy assuming – assuming we know about other people, assuming we know what they're thinking or feeling, so we're not even present. We're just inter-acting with our assumptions and stories. We're shadowboxing with illusions! We're not even there. This is why it makes good sense to ask ourselves again and again, how would we act if we just related to the man or woman who is standing before us instead of relating to our stories...? How...?

The answer is so obvious it hits us smack in the face. We'd act differently and be different. We'd be like little children, fresh and new. And there would be so much more love. This you know immediately if you try this exercise. It simply can't lead anywhere else because there's nowhere else to go! Without our stories, we would simply have to love everyone (including ourselves). We wouldn't be able to act otherwise. How could we? Because without stories, everything would be so strange and new that we would have to depend on ourselves and our own inner knowingness to deal with the present moment – to deal with any present moment.

All I can say is every time I try it; it feels like love!

Just think about it. If you couldn't tell your stories, how would it be with say your girl/boyfriend? Or with your friends?

Or your children? It would be a surprise every time wouldn't it? If you simply couldn't remember what had happened before, you'd be blown away at the wonder of all that is going on in every now moment.

When you allow yourself to try this out mentally, even for a few short minutes, you will discover how much happier you feel about everyone and everything – and how much more relaxed you are! Being present without our stories is instant relaxation. It just is. All tension and worry just fades away. It has to. Because where does tension and worry come from anyway? From our stories obviously...

When you see the mechanism and realize what's going on – you wonder why you didn't see it before, it's so obvious. And then you also see how you've been doing this all your life. You see how much mental energy we're all using all the time on all our stories... Shadowboxing with illusions and wearing ourselves out! Without our stories, what's left? Without the past (which is where?) what's left? Without the future (which is where?) what's left? Not much to be honest, except the present moment – in all its natural glory!

Moving away from the now

What actually happens when we tell a story? Well the very moment we tell a story about the now, we are moving away from it. Not that this is necessarily bad as I said before, but we are usually quite unaware of what we are doing and therefore we do not see that in that very moment, we may well be blocking the goodness of our own hearts and planting the seed of our own suffering.

Seeing without a filter

Here's another way of looking at it. Being fully present in the now-moment is like seeing without a filter. Because your stories actually act like a filter between you and what is. Without your story, as we have discovered, there is just seeing. The view. Life. Happiness.

For most of us, however, seeing directly like this is impossible except in very short glimpses. And it's pretty hard to describe in words too, especially since words so quickly become stories! Anyway, the words I am using right now are just pointers that hopefully will help you move in that direction – in the direction of the present moment, which is here now – with no filter.

Call it plain seeing – no story.

Call it plain seeing – without interpreting what's before you.

Call it just looking – without identifying with the thoughts that are arising in your mind.

Call it letting thoughts come and go naturally – with no attachment.

When we start playing around with these concepts, we discover sooner or later how our minds operate. We see that thoughts arise all by themselves; it has nothing to do with us! We're not involved at all! Thoughts just happen. They appear. They just do. This is the way of it. This is our nature. Or you could say, this is the nature of mind and there's nothing we can do about it. Not that there's anything inherently wrong with this or with the reality of thoughts arising. The problem, as I said before, is that we get so mental – so distracted by our thoughts of the past or future – so attached to our stories – that we miss the glory of the present moment and of our own natural happy state. The gift of life is right before us and we miss it over and over and over again. And then we frantically look everywhere else for the happiness that's right here.

That's why if you want to live a happy life, I highly recommend you stop up during the course of your day and just look. Experiment with this and briefly stop up in the stream of things and just look at what is. Look at what's in front of you and let things be.

It's an interesting experiment and the results can be quite

startling. At some point, if you keep bringing yourself back to this often enough, you will find that many of your old concepts begin to dissolve. And in my experience, a new clarity arises and brief moments of incredible peace.

Which makes life very simple and very sweet.

Indeed. In... deed...

And what more do you discover? You discover that reality is the man you call your partner standing before you with a smile on his face. What needs doing? You discover that reality is the child before you who is crying. What needs doing? You discover that reality is the telephone ringing on your desk or the dishes on the kitchen table. What needs doing?

When we are here now, dealing with the present moment, life is so much simpler. What needs doing becomes obvious so we do it. When we are present, what else can we do? And what else is there to do? And what can possibly prevent us from dealing kindly, wisely, and lovingly with what is before us?

> **Relate to the situation before you.**
> **Not your story of the past or your story of the future.**

All this, I realize, is very radical. Just the thought that we may not be relating to what's really happening in front us is a such mind bender that it can be hard to get your head around it. I know it is for me and I'm still exploring the ramifications of what it means to stop telling myself stories about the significance of the events that are unfolding before me in this now moment. I'm making progress (I think) because at least I can ask myself the question – do the events unfolding before me in fact have any significance at all, other than the significance I give them? I mean can they? Is it possible? Asking the question always makes me drop the whole idea of significance altogether and focus on just "seeing" instead.

Here's what I've found. When I succeed in making the shift from storytelling to plain seeing I experience a certain blankness – you could call it a space without language – and a wonderful sense of quiet that I find completely delicious. And then love arises. I can't tell you why, all I know is that it's just there. It's a powerful heartfelt feeling in this now moment that always leads to or is in itself spontaneous right action. I can't explain this either but everything feels quite natural – and quiet. And there's this knowingness – a feeling that you know what to do as if spontaneous right action just arises automatically because it's who we are. And also because that's all there is. This inborn wisdom that is us.

> **Happiness is not what you think.**

In one sense, when 'seeing' happens, it's as if we discover something that was always there – only we never noticed it. And we find that this 'whatever' is just moving right along, all the time with this inner knowingness that is us. And if this is the case – and it certainly seems to be – does it mean that this inner wisdom-knowingness in fact doesn't require anything whatsoever from us, even if we think that we have something to do with it?

If you ponder this long enough, you'll probably wake up one morning (like I did) and realize we don't have anything to do with any of it. It really is all moving along quite well without any help from us, regardless of what we might think or believe! (As if thinking could change one hair on our heads, as Jesus said). It's a rather startling and often disconcerting discovery, especially if we think we're important or in control! Now that's a big laugh isn't it! To discover that we don't have anything to do with any of it! To discover that it can take care of itself and us quite well, without any interference from us, and that in fact it works so much better if we just let it.

Ah and there's the hard part, the just 'letting'.

But if we can get the hang of it, the 'letting' is so relaxing compared to the constant struggle to maintain control over something that we can't possible have any control over in the first place. But of course most of us don't see it that way so we use enormous amounts of mental energy on a 'control' game we can never win.

The control game

So let's take a look at the control game for a minute. I used to think I was in control, do you? So the question is, are you? Am I? And if I am, what am I in control of?

Am I in control of my own body? Obviously not because why does it break down on me when I want it to function perfectly and why does it do stuff I don't really want it to do? And why does it live and breathe and do all kinds of things automatically, without any intention or participation on my part? I didn't ask my body to do this stuff and I can't stop it from doing it either. For example, it just breathes. It's not me who is doing this – I am just being breathed! The breathing is going on all by itself as so many other things in my body are, like my heart and digestion. The whole thing is just running on automatic. And the same goes for you.

And what about my mind? Am I in control of my mind? Now there's another big laugh, which will be obvious to you if you've ever tried to sit on your butt and meditate or follow your breathing without 'thinking' for just five minutes. It's a big joke right. Even the slightest flirt with meditation and breathing exercises will quickly teach you that you're definitely not in control of your mind no matter what you might have previously believed! The truth of the matter is your mind is all over the place and that thoughts are arising all the time. They just do. And that just happens to be the way of it. This is reality. Thoughts come and go and there's not much you can do about it even if you like to think you're the boss and you're in control. The truth of the matter is you're not! The truth is that mind is the way it is – for whatever reason. We are conscious – for whatever reason – and thoughts arise. And that's just how it is.

So tell me, where's the control? Are we actually in control of anything? It's a dizzying question for all us control freaks right!

The great Indian sage Sri Nisargadatta Maharaj said,

"Would people know that nothing can happen unless the entire universe makes it happen, they would achieve much more with less expenditure of energy."

From the book, *I Am That – Talks with Sri Nisargadatta Maharaj.*

So the real question is… are we doing anything?

Are you leaning?

When you start becoming aware that you're not in control of very much, you will probably discover many things – one of them is that you're 'leaning'. (Leaning goes hand in hand with the control game.) Now what do I mean by 'leaning'? Leaning is when we exert a whole lot of effort to achieve or do something over which we have no control whatsoever. Things happen or they don't but when we lean it's because we want a specific outcome. We want something to happen or not happen. The problem with leaning is that we're using so much energy yearning and striving for results and outcomes that are quite beyond our control. For example: You start a project and hope for success. You begin an assignment and hope your boss will like the job you do. You dress up pretty for a nice date and hope the guy will like the way you look. In every case, 'leaning' is going on. Why do I say that? Well because there are two parts to each of the above statements. Let's take a look at what I mean:

1. *You start a project and hope for success.* The fact is you're starting a project. Period. That's what's going on. You are going to do this or that to the very best of your ability. And you do. That's what's within your control. As for the results of your efforts, well forget about them. Results are way beyond our control. When you worry about results and success, you're leaning. Which isn't good for your peace of mind. The wise course is to do the best you can and leave the rest to the universe. Because that's the way it is anyway. The reality is that it's beyond your control no matter what you think or do. You have no control over any of it and by thinking you do, you cause yourself so much stress, worry and anguish.

2. *You begin an assignment and hope your boss will like the job you do.* Again, if you want to live a happy life, do the best you can and forget the rest. Don't worry about whether your boss will like what you do or not. Do your utmost and forget it. You have no control over what your boss thinks or doesn't think and if you use a lot of energy worrying about the results and hoping for approval, you are leaning and wearing yourself out for nothing!

3. *You dress up pretty for your date and hope the guy will like the way you look.* Again, this is like howling at the moon. Dress up as pretty as you can for your own pleasure and leave the rest to the universe. The guy is going to like/love you (or not like/love you) regardless of whether you're wearing eye makeup and your best dress. So if you want to enjoy your date, stop leaning and leave it to the universe. And remember, there's always another party going on somewhere in town.

Practice not leaning

All joking aside, is it possible not to lean? And if it is, can we practice not leaning? Yes I think it is possible, and like everything else in this book, it's all about becoming more aware of what we are doing. It's a process. It's about waking up and in this case, it's about learning to let things be. And here again I'd like to point out most emphatically that this has nothing to do with being passive or not caring or not doing your best. You should definitely do your best! You should definitely constantly check your intention and motivation. You should definitely go for the highest you can envision. But once you do your part, let it go. In other words, release the outcome instead of wanting and straining for specific results. Because this is where the struggle grinds you down. You could say it's a balance act, which involves doing your best and not wanting or caring about the results at the same time. Rather do and let go. Do and let things be. Is this possible? Of course it is! But it does take awareness and practice.

When we act, no matter what we do, we set in motion a chain of events. That's just the way it is. So if we act with the best possible intention and work for the very best we can envision, what more can we do? We're not running the show, even if we'd like to think we are. We're actually just here for the ride and it can be a very pleasant ride if we're not so attached to the results.

Success or failure, who cares? It's more about resting in yourself. She loves me, she loves me not, who cares? It's more about knowing your own worth and letting her go to find the love of her life (which might be you). My boss likes my work or he doesn't, who cares? It's more about showering your brilliance wherever you go and leaving it at that. If you win the prize, fine, if not, who cares? Brilliance is the way of it anyway.

Just as long as you let go, you'll be fine. It's the caring and worrying about outcomes that grinds us down.

So keep your intention pure.

Go for the gold and leave it at that.

This is a sure way to bring yourself back to this now moment and live a happy life.

Natural intelligence

This brings us full circle to the way of it again, which is the natural intelligence of life itself. If you sit back and watch it flow, you will discover that life seems to know exactly what to do all the time. It's just moving along quite quietly and it's self-regulating, too. Always seeking its own balance and always readjusting itself until at some point it can no longer maintain life in a particular form (body) anymore and then when that happens, that body falls away and life goes on taking on other forms. New bodies ever arising and passing away, always seeking balance and harmony.

Reality check

So let's stop for a moment and do a reality check. Where are you right now? Are you fully present, right here, reading this book? Or are you just partially here, while the rest of you is off shadow-boxing with illusions?

Now that I've got your attention, put the book down and see if you can see what is here now – with no story for a moment or two. Just see. You here, now. Sitting in chair. Book in hand. The reality of this moment. Can you relax and stay with this, with yourself, for a couple of minutes without pursuing the thoughts that naturally arise? Without getting absorbed in your stories? Because thoughts do arise, that is the nature of mind. But the question is can you allow these thoughts to arise and pass naturally... without following them, without identifying with them, and without getting absorbed in them? In other words, can you let the thoughts come and go while you just sit with yourself and breathe and allow yourself to be fully present in this now moment?

When I find this difficult to do (and sometimes it's more difficult than other times) I find it helps steady me to imagine that I am a mountain. I am a mountain, just sitting here, and the thoughts that are naturally arising in my mind are like small clouds floating by the mountaintop. The mountain, which is me, is not disturbed by the clouds, nor does the mountain get attached to the clouds, nor does the mountain do anything to get rid of the clouds. The mountain just sits and clouds just float by. And that's about it. Mountain and clouds. It's a nice way of anchoring yourself in this now moment.

So give it a try. Try being like a mountain and just sit... and let your thoughts naturally arise and float by.

If you practice doing this for a while you will discover that if there's no story about what happened before and no anticipation of what's coming, what is left? What is left when there's no story?

Now you see it, don't you? The utterly simple, entirely blissful, perfectly peaceful, and completely safe present moment that I keep talking about! The now and you in all its glory! Feels good doesn't it? Even if you can't stay in this space for very long without some practice, still it feels tremendously safe and excellent doesn't it?

So I ask you: If this isn't happiness, what is?

> **People think it's easy to do nothing, but in fact for most of us it's the most difficult thing in the world to do.**

Dealing with stressful emotions in this moment

So far in this chapter, we've only talked about dealing with so-called external situations and events, but what about internal events, i.e. what about dealing with our emotions, especially when they are unpleasant and stressful?

As you have discovered by now, the basic premise of this book is that nothing external can affect us and that it is our uninvestigated thoughts and stories that are the cause of our discomfort, suffering, fear and stressful emotions. This is because we cannot have an emotion without having a thought first – even though we are usually unaware of the thought (or story) that precedes an unpleasant emotion. Thus we find that all the powerful, unpleasant emotions we experience – such as fear, anxiety, anger, and sadness – arise as a result of our thoughts. An unpleasant emotion is just an alarm signal telling us there are thoughts or a story that are causing us anguish and that it is probably a good idea to investigate the thoughts or stories that are causing us so much distress. I believe that examining our thoughts, stories and underlying beliefs is the best and most effective way to release ourselves from unpleasant and conflicting emotions. But investigating these stories and under-lying beliefs can take time – in fact this can be a lifetime process for many of us. And during this process, discomfort and unpleasant emotions can still be very much a part of our lives. So the question is – when this happens – when stressful emotions arise – what is the best way to deal with these powerful emotions in the present moment? What is the best way to deal with these emotions until we have time to investigate the thoughts behind them and shine the light of truth on these thoughts and stories?

Fearing your emotions

Like many people, I've spent a lot of my life fearing my own emotions. I think many of us do this because we lack a tool to deal with them and because we believe our emotions are so powerful that they'll overwhelm us. So when powerful emotions arise, we are afraid because we think we'll be swept away and lose control. When we regard our emotions like this – like big ugly monsters that are going to devour us – we frantically try to suppress them or run away from them. But the more we run, the scarier they become. Unfortunately, fear and panic are not great ways of coping with stressful emotions because fear and panic just give extra energy to our distress and make everything seem worse. Of course, our fear and panic do not affect reality, but they do determine our experience of what's going on!

When I started to understand this mechanism, I began to look for new and better ways of coping with the powerful emotions I didn't understand and which triggered fear and panic in me. Over the years, as I watched myself scare myself over and over again, I began to discover that just being present and mindful of what was going on inside me (without interfering) was actually a more effective way of coping with my emotions than having a full-blown panic attack. And yes, I know this can be very difficult to do; but I found out that it can be learned. I found that we can make it our intention to be mindful and that the more we practice, the more mindful we become. When we get the hang of it, it changes everything.

> **Intention is everything.**

Watching what happens

So what exactly happens when you are mindful – when you are present and watch yourself when you're upset? In one way, it doesn't change anything – and in another way, it changes every-thing. Being mindful doesn't change the discomfort or fear or sadness you feel. They are still there. And the discomfort or fear or sadness still feels unpleasant and uncomfortable. But when you are mindful, you are more identified with the witness (with watching) and thus you create a certain distance to your distress. When this happens, you discover that you *can* allow your strong emotions and sensations to surface and run their course (decom-press) without going to pieces. And this discovery – that we can allow our feelings to arise and dissipate, and survive – changes everything for us.

When we realize that we can watch ourselves and our own worst fears from a distance, a shift in consciousness takes place, which slowly releases us from the iron grip of these emotions.

We discover that there is something about us that is greater than our fears; something about us that can embrace and live with and through the thoughts and emotions we find so terrifying. It's a very liberating discovery, even though it usually doesn't happen overnight. At least it didn't for me. It requires awareness. It takes practice. It takes your powerful intention. So don't be discouraged if you decide to be mindful and don't find immediate relief. And remember, wanting immediate relief is wanting and expecting a result, which is 'leaning', instead of just allowing yourself to be with your own discomfort and fear. In this case, like in all the other areas of our lives, wanting to feel better (leaning) often prevents us from feeling better! (We try so hard that we tend to push things away from us!)

It's also important to notice and understand that we actually make the situation a lot worse by trying to suppress our feelings. When we try to suppress how we really feel – we actually give these so-called "negative" emotions more power and intensity. That's the irony of it. When we try to suppress them, it's like keeping all these feelings under the tight lid of a pressure cooker – the steam just builds and builds. So it's pretty liberating when you realize that by allowing your feelings to surface and not resisting them – your feelings will come up and then pass. In a way it's like letting the steam out of a pressure cooker. When you don't resist your feelings, you take the steam out of them and then they're no longer so powerful, until finally they simply dissolve back into the nothingness from which they came.

Seeing not doing

So how do you do this in practice? How do you actually become mindful when you're upset or afraid? Well once you make the decision to be there for yourself, you do just that. You just sit and watch yourself. Or you just walk and watch yourself. Or you just lie down and watch yourself. In other words, you pay attention to you. You become aware. But you don't *do* anything. You just let everything unfold. Without trying to change anything. Without judging what you are observing. Without labeling what you are feeling as good or bad, you watch your emotions, feelings, and sensations unfold.

You let things be as they are.

You allow things to happen as they are happening.

You resist nothing.

This is seeing but not doing.

If you never tried this before, you will find that watching like this – being aware – being mindful – being present with yourself – is an extremely powerful experience. In practice it translates into being the kind, wise mother for yourself, the kind, wise mother who is lovingly watching over her fearful child. Only now you are both. You are both the watchful mother and the fearful little child at the same time. When you are mindful in this way, you are in fact shifting your focus from the fearful, little child part of you to the wise, watchful mother part. And then as the wise mother, you just watch the fearful part of you and meet yourself with love and understanding. And just like any wise, watchful mother, your wisdom nature will realize that you can't make the scary feelings go away by resisting them, but you can be there for yourself. You can comfort you. You can hold you.

Resisting doesn't work

So life teaches us that we cannot be released from powerful, stressful emotions by resisting, ignoring, or repressing them – no matter how hard we try. In fact, life teaches us just the opposite. We learn from experience that resisting, repressing and ignoring unpleasant emotions just tend to make things worse.

When we learn the secret of mindfulness, we learn that instead of running away and feeling threatened by powerful emotions, we can just sit with them and breathe and allow them to be. Because mindfulness is peaceful, like a great calm ocean where the powerful waves of emotion can arise and thrash about, but do no damage. If this sounds like meditation to you, it is. Mindfulness is a kind of meditation. This awareness, this sitting with yourself and not doing anything and not expecting anything to happen is what meditation is all about. And so is feeling that you don't have to achieve anything at all.

So you just sit and breathe and watch your emotions come and go. And you do absolutely nothing about any of it. As we practice this and learn to let things be, we gradually start to desensitize ourselves to our fear of our own feelings. These tactics or techniques – mindfulness, observation, meditation – slowly and gradually release us from our own mistaken belief that our own emotions can somehow be dangerous to us. And if we combine this practice with the powerful technique of investigating our stories as described in Chapter No. 4, over time we will find ourselves released from the grip of many of the highly charged emotions we fear so much. And in the end, life becomes a much kinder place to be.

The intention to be awake

So whether we're talking about internal or external events, to be present and deal with what is really in front of you, you must be awake. And if you're not awake, the only way to get there is to have the intention to be awake. Intention is everything. So be earnest and intend! Intend to be awake in this now moment. Intend to be mindful and see what is without interfering or inter-preting or trying to understand. And be earnest about it.

Intend to see without judging. Intend to drop your opinions. Intend to be here now and experience the fluidity of this moment as it is, and sooner or later, you will!

Intend to keep bringing yourself back to the present now moment without commenting on it or explaining it to yourself. And if you slip away, as you most certainly will, come back and intend again. And keep practicing. And intend again. Intention requires constant vigilance. Nothing less will do.

Intend to be awake over and over again. And then intend again. And each time you discover you're not present but off somewhere in your mind conversing with your girlfriend or your father or your boss, bring yourself back to the now. And intend again.

Keep intending to be here now.

If you are earnest and this is your honest intention, you will discover that you can practice 'seeing' at any moment during the course of your day – no matter what you are doing. Just do it. Decide to be present and mindful when you are washing the dishes. Decide to be present and mindful when you are driving your car. Decide to be present and mindful when you are with your partner. And then watch. And watch again and decide to see what you are doing and what is going on – and you will.

You can also take specific time-outs during the course of your day to practice 'seeing'. You can, for example, start by just sitting in your chair and practicing 'seeing' as described above for five minutes. If you do this regularly – once or twice a day for just a few minutes each time – you will soon get the knack of it. It's almost like learning to ride a bicycle. It takes a bit of practice, but pretty soon you will get it. And then 'seeing' will start to happen for you naturally – and who knows what you will see!

> **You cannot remain asleep if your intention is to wake up. Intention is everything.**

Happiness is the now

One of the things we discover when we are mindful is that happiness is the now. Where else could it be?

And we also discover that happiness now is our true nature. How do I arrive at this startling conclusion? It's simple. All the exercises in this book – as you have discovered by now – are all different ways of 'seeing' and 'being' in the present moment. And when you do this, you discover two things. First of all you discover that *you are the now*. Why is this so? Well it has to be. Just ask yourself – what is the now? The now is what you are. The now is where you are. The now is you... it has to be. What else could the now be, but you? Think about it. Without you, there would be no now!

So let this sink in for a moment. *You are the now.*

The second thing you find out is that when you are mindful and fully present, the experience of the now is utterly simple, entirely blissful, perfectly peaceful, and completely safe. Which is a pretty good definition of happiness isn't it!

Now this is a very important discovery because it means – despite what you may think at the moment – that you cannot do anything to make yourself happy because you already are happiness itself. Happiness is your nature – because *you are the now*! And the now is utterly simple, entirely blissful, perfectly peaceful and completely safe.

When I contemplate this, I can come to no other conclusion than that you, the now and happiness are all one and the same! They are equal, identical and interchangeable – or all one – however you want to look at it. This I find is a pretty amazing discovery. To realize that this is who/what we are – and that happiness is our true nature. The icing on the cake is that there's only one place we can experience the happiness that we are – and that's right here now.

> **There is only one place you can be happy –**
> **and it's here and now.**

Unconditional happiness

The happiness I am talking about now is true happiness of course, the happiness that is totally independent of outer conditions. You can call this happiness – unconditional happiness. This is the type of happiness that no job, no amount of money in your bank account, no lover, no guru, no success or amount of fame can bring you. When you are happy because of outside circumstances, conditions or events – your happiness is conditional and based on value judgments, belief systems, and stories. Not that there is anything wrong with conditional happiness, but it is important to realize that when our happiness is conditional, sooner or later it will disappear because it is dependent on and triggered by external events and circumstances which will and do change.

The happiness you experience in the present moment when you are mindful, is your true nature. It's unconditional because it depends on no one or thing. It's who you are.

A good exercise

Thich Nhat Hanh has this wonderful poem/exercise that we can use to help us be mindful and experience the happiness of being fully present in this now moment. It goes like this:

"I have arrived, I am home
In the here, in the now."

He suggests we use the first sentence as a breathing exercise to help bring us back to the present moment when we get distracted and forget. All you have to do is say "I have arrived," on the in-breath and "I am home," on the out-breath. It's a wonderful exercise and brings an immediate sense of peace and happiness. When you do it, you will find yourself relaxing and discover that you are here now in the present moment. You can use this poem when you are sitting in your chair as a kind of meditation practice or you can say it to yourself at intervals during the course of your day, while you are walking or waiting in line or doing the dishes or working. No matter when or where you use this little poem, you will discover it makes you feel good. And this is because wherever you are and whatever you are doing, you already have arrived at your true home, which is the present moment – the now.

Welcome home!

Happiness is your nature. It's who you are.

Know what is what

> **The number 9 cause of suffering and unhappiness is wanting absolute satisfaction from relative experiences.**

We get in trouble – over and over again – because we don't know what is what. And since we don't know what is what, we want (and expect) absolute satisfaction from relative things and experiences. And this is impossible.

And since we don't know what is what, we give only relative importance to the absolute. And we get in trouble again – over and over again.

But fortunately for us, it's all in our minds so it doesn't make any difference at all to the absolute what we think! And when you understand this, you're home free! Absolutely free! And that's what we all want, isn't it? To be home, free. Absolutely and positively home free now and forever.

Only by gazing directly into the face of the absolute can you get it. And if this sounds like high mysticism to you, it isn't. In fact, it's the most practical thing I can tell you. The most practical thing in this wild experience we call life, even though you can't understand a word of it.

You may not be able to understand it, but you can know it.

You want absolute satisfaction from your house, your car, your wife, your job, and it's a hopeless battle. Everything you are attaching yourself to is disappearing right before your very eyes so no wonder you're screaming in broad daylight. No wonder the bombs are falling. No wonder there's pain on the inside and out.

There's only one place where absolute satisfaction can be found. Only one place; but no one's taught us where to look – so we don't know how. We don't even know why. All we know is we're howling, howling for satisfaction that never comes.

In the land with no mirrors – a parable

In the land with no mirrors, no one knows what they look like. In the land with no mirrors, no one has ever seen their own face, including you. In the land with no mirrors, even you have never seen your own face. So you have no idea what you look like. You have no idea who you are.

And that's what it's like for most of us. We're wandering around like the people in the land with no mirrors. Wondering who we are and what we look like because we've never seen our own faces.

So it's a great mystery to us. And we're longing to know our true nature.

Then every once in a while, someone comes along and holds a mirror up for us to see. But since we've never seen our own faces before, when this strange and wondrous being holds up a mirror for us to see, we don't recognize ourselves – even though it's us. Even though we're looking right at our very own faces.

It's the same with reality – with our own true nature. We're so ignorant of our own true nature that even when someone holds up a mirror for us, we don't get it. We don't recognize ourselves.

So we continue our wandering, howling at the moon.

But here's the mirror. It's right in front of you. Reality is right here. Reality is right now. Reality is this moment, us. Can you recognize it when you see it — because here's the mirror! Now is the time to look even if you don't understand what you see.

Because you can't understand. Because it — reality — is beyond language, which makes it inconceivable. But still it's right here now.

Words and language are the building blocks of concepts. And concepts are the mental cages we trap ourselves in. The mental cages we build that keep us from seeing. Outside the cages is life. Free life. And love. Vast and unimaginable.

But we are so innocent that we believe our own words, thoughts and concepts! We believe them even though thoughts, words and concepts are not real. They are just what they are. Words, thoughts and concepts. They have no life of their own, no substance, no reality, none whatsoever. But we give them life by believing them. We give them life by identifying with them. But they are nothing.

And nothing else is going on.

When you stop believing your thoughts and concepts — even for just a moment — the incredible happens and your old world cracks. Leaving you blank. And without your concepts, you may feel yourself falling through the cracks of the universe. But it's a free fall and absolutely safe — so don't be afraid.

In that moment, you discover something else. You discover that you are still alive and that all your words, thoughts and concepts only occupy a very small space in your consciousness. Very small. And that's okay too because in that very small space, they seem quite capable of taking care of themselves. Without any interference or help from you.

Beyond that, the rest is the real. The wordless real.

And this real, which is now, is the face of the absolute – and it's always here now. Staring at you/you staring at it/you being it/it being you. One and the same – beyond language. And it's all happening simultaneously with all your relative stuff. It's all happening simultaneously with the house and the car and the television and the girlfriend. The absolute is staring you in the face all the time. But how often do you see it? How often do you even look? How often does your gaze see through and beyond your girlfriend and the television? How often do you recognize the gaze of the absolute staring you in the face? How often?

Actually I believe we have this experience all the time. Or at least more often than we might suspect. But we don't recognize it. We don't recognize the utter blankness or bliss of an experience that is beyond language and beyond our concepts – so we overlook it. Or you could say, not recognizing it, we miss it completely.

Because you see, we're the people in the land with no mirrors. And in the land where we dwell, with no mirrors, we don't recognize reality when we see it.

> **Because we don't know what reality is –
> we don't recognize it when we see it.**

So a word of caution – about everything, including everything I am saying in this book too – when you seek absolute satisfaction from the relative, when you seek absolute satisfaction from your words, thoughts, concepts, from your job, house, relationship, from your past, future or whatever, you are setting yourself up for failure. Relative pleasures give relative satisfaction. Well and good and please enjoy. Relative troubles give relative discomfort. Well and good and know that they too will pass. Because sooner or later, everything passes. Everything in the relative world changes and becomes everything else in the relative world. That is the way of it. Sooner or later.

Only the absolute remains the absolute and can give you absolute satisfaction.

> **Only the absolute can give you absolute satisfaction.**

But... now that we've gazed at the absolute for a moment, let's go back to the relative world and play some more...

No. 10

Learn to see beyond impermanence

> **The number 10 cause of suffering and unhappiness is believing we become nothing.**

Death and dying can be pretty scary things to think about – but since death is a part of life, learning to deal with it must also be a part of living a happy life.

I believe that moving the focus back and forth between the relative and the absolute is what makes this book interesting. Even though most of the book is dedicated to exploring how we deal with our experiences in the relative world we are living in, it is the absolute perspective that offers a new perspective to dealing with the relative world. The absolute puts a different spin on things – because everything is seen from a different point of view – and this is true when we contemplate death too. As far as I can see, the absolute perspective is what makes it possible for us to contemplate death at all because it gives us a sense of comfort. When you contemplate death from the relative perspective, it's just too frightening and depressing. From a relative point of view, all we can say is that we're all going to die and that we're all going to lose everyone we love and everything we care about. What can be more scary and depressing than that? So the only place we can seek and find real comfort is in the absolute perspective – and that's basically what all spirituality and religion are about. Trying to get a perspective that makes it possible to live a happy life in the face of death and imperma-nence in the relative world. Because we all are going to have to face this issue – sooner or later.

So here are some of the comforting ways I believe we can contemplate our own approaching deaths.

Is death dangerous?

The idea that 'death is dangerous' is an idea that haunts most of us. We are afraid of death because of this idea, so let's consider it.

Let's ask ourselves – is death dangerous?

And if we answer yes, which we probably will, let's ask ourselves – where's the proof? Is there any proof that death is dangerous?

The fact that people die, that everyone dies, doesn't prove that death is dangerous, does it? All it proves is that death happens. But we really don't know if dying is dangerous at all. Because no one has ever come back from the dead and told us, have they? So where's the proof? Where's the proof that death is dangerous?

In reality, there's no proof at all. No evidence whatsoever that death is dangerous. No objective facts to support the idea that death is dangerous.

All we can say for sure is that death happens and the rest we don't know. That's reality. That's what we know.

So what are we afraid of?

We're afraid of the thought. We're afraid of the thought 'death is dangerous'. That's what we're afraid of because we don't really know about death itself.

So let me ask you the question: Who would you be without the thought that 'death is dangerous'?

How would you feel? How would you feel if you couldn't think the thought 'death is dangerous'?

Go inside and ask yourself this question and allow yourself to answer it honestly. Just for yourself. Be free and answer it and then sit with your answer. And feel it.

And when you have your answer, ask yourself how would you live your life if you didn't and couldn't believe the thought 'death is dangerous'?

When I do this and try to imagine how I'd feel if I didn't believe the thought 'death is dangerous', I discover a radical shift going on inside me. First of all, everything in me just relaxes. And then I feel peace – a deep sense of peace. So I find it very comforting to just sit with this feeling for a while.

Is life dangerous?

Since playing with thoughts is the best way to set yourself free, here's another thought to play with. Ask yourself: If death isn't dangerous, how can life be dangerous? I ask this question now because I believe the two are irrevocably linked together. If you are afraid of death, you must be afraid of life too.

The connection is obvious. If you're afraid of death, you're afraid of life because you think something might happen to you. And if something happens to you, you could die! But if death isn't dangerous, what then? What can happen? So without the fear of death, how can life be dangerous? What could possibly happen to you? Where could you possibly go or fall? Well you say, you could die... and so? If death isn't dangerous, so what?

And if this is true, it leads us to the next outrageous thought, which is – how can anything in life be dangerous if life itself isn't dangerous?

These are liberating and intoxicating questions to play with – because just asking helps us to break out of the cage of fear that binds us. I find there's nothing better than sitting quietly with these questions and answering them as often as possible – and then really allowing myself to feel the answers inside me. Each time I do, something miraculous happens because nothing is more comforting than this. Nothing is more comforting than waking up and seeing what is real.

Asking questions like this is something you can do for yourself too. You can get yourself to this place – to this state of seeing – by asking yourself what you know for sure. When you do this, you will probably discover the same thing I discovered

– that you don't know very much at all – at least not for sure. And that you absolutely don't know if dying is dangerous either, which is like snowflakes of pure grace falling ever so gently upon you because it allows you to live so much more freely and sanely and happily and authentically and lovingly. So ask yourself...

Take every ancient scary thought and bring it to the awakened one inside you – and see what happens!

Great comfort

Here's something else we can do when we are afraid of death, which I believe can bring us great comfort. We can think about, meditate on, and truly try to understand the truth of the statement *'something cannot become nothing'*.

Why is this statement – *something cannot become nothing* – such a great comfort? To answer this, we must look at what the statement means. It means literally what it says – something cannot become no-thing. This is because nothing is – no-thing. No-thing is non-existent. No-thing has no substance. It's nowhere. So something, which is some thing, which has substance – cannot become no-thing or non-existent. Where would it go? Modern science has confirmed this. Modern science tells us that matter cannot be destroyed. Science has demonstrated that matter can and does change form all the time and that matter also becomes energy, but matter does not and cannot disappear. In other words, matter cannot be destroyed. Matter and energy are interchangeable but they don't disappear. They don't become no-thing. Again, how could they? Where would they go? They cannot go no-where since there is no no-where.

So we see that it is impossible for something to disappear and become no-thing. We see that existence and life itself are a closed loop. When something exists, it continues to exist in one form or another – or as energy. We cannot explain why this is so, but when we look deeply at reality, we see that this is the truth of what is going on. And here it is important to state again, 'seeing' reality means seeing what is – even if you cannot understand what you are 'seeing' or explain *why* it is.

So when we look at reality, we 'see' (and experience) that something is and because something is, we also know that it cannot be destroyed. Something always remains something – though it can and does change form.

We are also 'something' so this must hold true of us too.

And since we are 'something', we cannot become no-thing.

This is a very comforting thought, indeed.

Something cannot become nothing.

And there's another aspect to this. If something cannot become no-thing, we can also see that no-thing cannot become something. That too we find is impossible. And again, this can be confusing because we cannot explain *why* this is so – but we can know that it is the reality of this thing we call life. Life cannot arise from no-thing since it is something.

Where do we go?

I find it helps a lot to think about this because when we examine what we are – we must come to the conclusion that we are something because we know we exist. This is our experience, our reality. We experience that we are. And since we are, we must be something and since we are something it means we cannot become nothing. This is impossible. Life and science have proven that this is true whether we understand it or not.

Since we are some-thing, we cannot become no-thing. Again

where would we go?

It is very comforting to meditate on this truth because so many of us equate what we call 'death' with 'nothingness'. We equate dying with total extinction – with annihilation – with falling into a black hole of nothingness. But in light of the above, we have to ask ourselves is it true? When we die, where do we go? Do we become nothing? Do we become non-existent? The answer must be no, we do not become nothing because this is impossible.

It is true that we cease to exist in this form, as this body – this is obvious. We see with our own eyes that bodies come and go. But the question is where do we go when we no longer are this body? What happens to the life that we are when this body no longer manifests itself? I cannot answer this question, but when I contemplate the above truths, I can see that we must continue to exist in some form or other – or as energy. This must be true because we know that something cannot be destroyed and become no-thing, something can only change form and become something else. This I find most comforting to think about.

Where did you begin?

Here's another interesting way of looking at it. You can ask yourself – where did you begin? If you answer oh I began on the day of my birth, please ask yourself if this is really true. Did you really begin on the day of your birth? Did you suddenly appear from nowhere and no-thing on that very day? And you have to answer of course not. You have to answer that before the day you were born you were also alive and well in your mother's stomach. So you cannot truthfully say you began on the day you were born. And before the nine months you spent in your mother's stomach, where were you then? You were in her egg and in your father's sperm and then this sperm and egg came together and grew in your mother's stomach. And before that, before your mother's egg and your father's sperm, before your mother and your father were even born, where were you then? Where you not in your parents' parents and in their parents and in all those who came before them? Your DNA proves that you were.

And if you look closely you will find that you were more than that. Look closely and you can also see that you must also be the food your mother was eating every day she carried you in her stomach because that food was everyday becoming you as you grew into the you-baby that was born nine months later. And also, when you see this, you can see another thing – that the food she was eating, which was becoming you, was becoming the food it was becoming because the sun was shining and the rain was falling and the rich soil was bringing it forth. So you cannot truthfully say that you in fact are not the sun and the rain and the earth that brought forth the food that became you, can you? So where did you come from? Where did you begin?

What will you become?

In the same way as we can ask ourselves where we began, we can also ask ourselves what we will become when this body is no longer this body. Where will we go? Will we become the good earth, the wind in the tress, the flowers and the grass, and the clouds above? Will we be in the ocean or in the smile of our great-great-grandchildren? Think about it for a minute. Where will we go and what will we become? Since we cannot see or know where we began, how can we see or know where we will end? Perhaps this isn't even the right question to ask. Perhaps beginning and ending have nothing to do with reality. Because in reality, we simply cannot see beginnings or endings nor can we conceive of them. Perhaps it is more truthful to ask, considering what we truly 'see' when we look closely, did we ever begin and will we ever end?

> **Since you are the result of everything
> that's ever happened,
> perhaps you are everything that's ever happened.**

Where does this leave us?

It leaves us, I believe, right back where we started this book – with the basic premise that since all our experiences are thoughts in our minds, *all suffering is mental.*

Which brings us back to mind and the nature of mind.

Because the nature of mind holds the key to living a happy life!

If all suffering is mental, then only by looking at our minds and how they work, can we begin to understand how we make ourselves suffer.

What is mind?

When you contemplate mind and ask yourself what is mind, you discover, if you're honest with yourself, that mind is the most mysterious thing of all. What is it? Where is it? How can you even define it? Mind is like the wind. Who knows what it is? Who can tell you? Who's the expert? Whom can you trust? And how does what other people say measure up to your own experience?

Have you ever watched your mind? Really watched it? And if you have, what happens when you try to watch your mind? Is it easy to do or does watching your mind take practice? And when you watch it, can you catch it?

Many people throughout the ages have asked these questions and many have tried to watch their minds and answer these questions. So there are many answers and lots of speculation about these matters. So whom do you believe? And where's the proof? When it comes to understanding the nature of mind, is there anyone or anything you can trust more than your own experience?

Here's one way of looking at it: Since we all have mind and all are mind, each one of us is endowed with this magical mystical quality we call mind. Each one of us has mind. This must mean that each one of us is fully capable of exploring the phenomenon we call mind. Each and every one of us is fully equipped. No one is better or worse off in the game called mind. We're all equal. No matter how rich or poor, young or old, high or low you are, each one of us is endowed with this magical mystical quality we call mind. And it's free. Absolutely free! Nowhere and everywhere.

Mind.

So let's play with our mind.

Let's play with being mindful of mind.

Mindful of mind.

Taking a look at mind.

Watching mind.

Minding mind.

What is mind...? What is it? And what is the difference between what we call mind and what we call consciousness?

There are many definitions – and different traditions and different teachers use these words differently. Here is how I am using the words:

Consciousness is naked awareness, the ground or background upon which everything exists. Consciousness is the ability to be aware, to know, the ability to watch and witness. Consciousness is the state before, beyond, around, behind and after thought (and the use of language). Consciousness contains mind, which I define as the phenomenon of thoughts arising in consciousness. When I talk about consciousness I mean the naked awareness beyond thought.

Mind is like the wind

Mind – the phenomenon of thoughts arising – is like the wind because you just can't catch it. You can't hold onto it. You can't pin it down or tame it. So it's difficult to get a handle on it. Mind (or thoughts arising) just comes and goes, whenever it wants to or so it seems.

So what is this phenomenon?

No one has ever been able to tell us exactly what it is.

No one has ever been able to bottle it and hold it up before us and say, "Look, this is mind! This is what it is."

So the only thing we can do is watch it.

This is what we can do, each and every one of us. We can watch our minds.

We can sit quietly and watch our minds.

Or we can run around and watch our minds.

Or we can be busy and watch our minds.

But we always have this ability (whether we know it or not) to watch and observe and witness our minds and see what's going on. This is something we are all capable of doing if we want to. If this is our intention, mind can be watched. And we can get better at watching mind too. But it takes practice.

This is because we basically have two types of awareness. We have the automatic awareness, in other words we are conscious and we live and think and do things quite automatically. And then we also have the ability to be conscious of the fact that we are conscious. In other words, we have the ability to be aware of being aware. We can watch our minds and we can watch our awareness. We can observe and witness our minds and we can observe and look back at the witnessing consciousness itself. But it takes practice.

Watching your mind

One way of watching your mind is to just sit and breathe and watch yourself. This means to withdraw your attention from outer things and turn your attention inward. When we do this for a while, we come face to face with the nature of our minds. The first thing we discover is that it is impossible to just sit and not think. We just can't do it.

So immediately when we sit, we discover that thoughts automatically arise. That's just the way it is. That is the first lesson in the nature of mind – thoughts arise. They just do. And nothing we can do can prevent thoughts from arising. When we watch like this, we discover that we have absolutely nothing to do with the process. It just happens.

Thoughts arising

And here we come to the core of our experience of this life because we discover that as thoughts arise, our world arises too. That's just the way it is.

It's something like this. Have you ever experienced waking up in the morning and being a total blank? I am sure you have because this is something we all experience on occasion. You wake up and you know you are awake but there is no thought and no world. You are blank. You can't quite remember who you are or where you are or even what you are. And then, in a split second, it comes back to you. The thoughts come tumbling in and your world appears. You are this person in this bed with this mate beside you and with this job to go to in a little while. And so it goes. With the thoughts, your world appears again.

This is the whole of it.

The whole of life, the whole of our life experience, is like that. Only we usually don't see it happening because it happens so quickly. But this is what's going on in every now moment – thought/world appearing simultaneously. Before the thought, there was no world. And if you make yourself very quiet and watch very carefully and long enough, you might be able to see this. You might be able to discover for yourself that this is true. But don't believe me; test it for yourself.

And it may even happen that when this happens and you begin to see, you may also be able to see what was there before the thought arose – in that split second of no time – that is if you sit quietly enough and watch carefully enough. Because what was there before a thought arose? Can you find that moment, that place, that space within yourself? Moment, place, space, there is no word to describe it... And what about what is after a thought? Right before the next thought arises. Can you find that place, space, moment? Watch and ask yourself. Go within and look. It is there. Can you find out? *Can you see what is before a thought? And what is after a thought?* What is it like? How does it feel? And does it look or feel like anything? What is your experience? What do you see?

This is what meditation is – sitting quietly by yourself, with yourself, and watching. Not doing anything in particular, not wanting anything in particular, just watching. Not interfering, just watching. Who are you without your thoughts? Can you find that moment? That place? That experience? What is your life without your thoughts? Who would you be without the thoughts that are arising, without untamed mind bubbling up, like a well within you creating stars and worlds and experiences for you to frolic and play with?

Seeing behind impermanence

Did you get a glimpse of before or after thoughts arising? Because as we now discover, the thoughts arising are your life experience and since thought itself is impermanent, so is your life experience. This is a big discovery and it's something you will discover for yourself if you sit long enough. This is just the way of it. As thoughts arise, your life in the world arises. They go together or you could say they are one and the same. And because thoughts are as impermanent as the wind, so too is your life. One and the same and both as impermanent as the coming and going of the wind.

But the glimpse of before, after, or between thought – did you see it for what it is? Did you see it for a moment and experience it? Did you see what is before thought, behind thought, between thought, after thought? Did you notice the gap in between the thoughts? Like the moment of powerful orgasm when you just are – totally blown away – being or existing beyond thought. Can you glimpse it?

No thought but just being.

No thought but you are still here.

Existence.

No thought but still something is. Some experience, something beyond words, because again words are descriptions of thoughts and thoughts cannot describe what is beyond them... thoughts/words cannot describe what is beyond, behind, before, around impermanence...

Here we have what the wise ones have been telling us all along. Behind the magical mystical dance of impermanence that we think is so real and which gives us so much suffering and so much pleasure, something is. Something that is beyond the thoughts and words. Something that words cannot describe because thoughts cannot go there. In fact, thoughts can only distract us from seeing what exists beyond and behind the dance of impermanence, because we mistake our passing thoughts for reality and miss the real.

When we wake up, we discover that our thoughts are not reality. They are just thoughts. They are just the bubbling well, dancing and changing right before our eyes.

But the real is beyond the bubbling well... the real is beyond what any words can tell. And so we reach the point where you have to go it alone and find out for yourself. Words can take you no further, they can only suggest, they can only point the way. The rest is up to you. Only you can go to the edge of the river of life and test these things for yourself.

And so this is my final suggestion if you want to live a happy life. Check this out for yourself. Test it. Find out for yourself. Learn to see what's beyond... Nothing is more important if you want to live a happy life! Nothing.

The joy of it

Once you get over the shock of finding out that you have absolutely nothing whatsoever to do with this magical mystical quality we call mind, can you do anything but love it? Can you do anything but fall down on your knees and praise the greatness that has somehow brought about all this wonder and joy that is given to us in every now moment? Is any other reaction possible – past all your suffering and all your joy and laughter? What is left? Who can you be? Beyond all suffering and all pleasure? What can you be, beyond the thoughts that are arising? What is there in this territory beyond words? Beyond conception? Beyond space and time? Who and what and where? And still you find you exist, but not perhaps the self you once conceived yourself to be. But a beingness that is beyond describing. A peace that is beyond understanding. A love that is beyond imagining…

And when you discover this, what is there left to do but…

Dream, play and have a happy life!

> **Dream, play and have a happy life!**

A Happy Life Worksheet

The Practical Application

To help you remember and integrate the ideas in this book into your daily life, I suggest thinking about these ideas and working with them on a daily basis until they begin to bear fruit in your consciousness. So I encourage you to work with how each of the 10 ways applies to your life.

I developed the following 2-step exercise to help:

The 2 Steps

Step 1: Explore your life

The 10 ways are listed on the following pages. After each way, there is a blank page where you can write down the different ways or areas in your life where you are having difficulty with the suggested concept. Sit quietly with yourself and write down everything that comes to mind. Don't censor yourself, for best results write down freely everything that comes to mind.

For example, under "Investigate your stories" you might write down things like: "I tell myself scary stories about what will happen to me if I don't fully recover from this operation." Or "I worry a lot about my children's future." Or "I think a lot about what I will do when I get older if I lose the money I invested on the stock market."

Step 2: Enjoy your happy life

As you work with these ideas and progress and develop, it is a good idea to again sit with yourself and go through the 10 ways one more time. But this time, allow yourself to see and feel who you would be if you no longer thought and did the things that are at present preventing you from experiencing a happy life. In other words, simply sit and see yourself, doing, being, feeling and living each of the 10 ways in your daily life. This can really open your mind to a new vision of yourself and help you develop the flexibility of mind that makes life a joy to live!

No. 1
Accept what is

> **The number 1 cause of suffering and unhappiness is
> wanting life to be something it's not.**

Step 1:
Write here the ways in which you are resisting reality in your life.
If, for example, you are ill or handicapped in some way and all
the time feeling bad because of this, write this down because you
are resisting the reality of your own situation. Write down as
many examples as come to mind of where and how you are
resisting the way your life is.

Step 2:
Write down and envision how you would feel, live, be if you
were no longer resisting reality and comparing yourself to some
impossible standard in these areas of your life.

No. 2
Want what you have

> **The number 2 cause of suffering and unhappiness is wanting what you don't have.**

Step 1:

Write here the all the things you don't have that you think you need to live a happy life. What is lacking right now in your life? What is it about your present situation that is preventing you from living a happy life? What is it that's not good enough at this moment? Why do you need these things? How will they make you happy? Are you sure they will make you happy?

Step 2:

Try to describe and then envision how you would feel and be if you wanted exactly what you have at this present moment. How would you live your life if everything you have at this very moment was perfect for you? How would it feel?

No. 3
Be honest with yourself

The number 3 cause of suffering and unhappiness is not communicating honestly with yourself.

Step 1:

List here the situations when and where you are not communicating honestly with yourself. This is not difficult to find out. Almost every situation where you feel discomfort is a situation where you have not been honest with yourself about what you feel and want. Get in touch with your inner voice and answer this question as honestly as you can.

Step 2:

Write down and envision how it would feel if you were communicating honestly with yourself. How you would live your life if you were honest with yourself? What would you do differently? What would you tell other people that you're not telling them now? And what about the ways in which you communicate with others? How would this change?

No. 4
Investigate your stories

> **The number 4 cause of suffering and unhappiness
> are the scary stories you tell yourself
> about life and the world.**

Step 1:

What stories are you telling yourself that are making you unhappy right now? Be specific and write down the main things that are making you feel unhappy. When you identify the areas in your life where you feel discomfort or unhappiness – be it in your relationships or at work or with your family – you will find you are telling yourself a story about these people or situations. So write the story down as clearly as you can. What are the 'shoulds'?

Step 2:

Write down and envision how you would feel in these different situations and relationships if you didn't have your stories about these people and situations. Allow yourself to experience how it would be if you simply couldn't remember your stories. Let go and expand your mind. How would life be without your 'shoulds'?

No. 5
Mind your own business

The number 5 cause of suffering and unhappiness is minding other people's business.

Step 1:
Write down here whose business you are minding. Are you minding your children's business? Your partner's? Your friends'? Are you projecting and overextending yourself? Write down as honestly as you can the situations that come to mind where you may be minding other people's business.

Step 2:
Sit quietly and envision how it would feel if you pulled back your projections about the people you mentioned above and just stayed home with yourself. Write it down too. How does it feel to set other people free? To know in your heart that they are perfectly capable of taking care of themselves and that you love and support them regardless of their choices in life. Sit with these ideas for a while and let them sink in.

No. 6
Follow your passion and accept the consequences

> **The number 6 cause of suffering and unhappiness is not doing what you want because you think people will disapprove.**

Step 1:

What is your true passion in life? Write it down! Say it out loud to yourself. What is it you want to do more than anything else in the world? What makes your heart sing? It's not a question here of whether you can do it or not, just write down what it is. Get clear with yourself about what is your heart's desire. Be honest!

Step 2:

Write down and envision how it would feel to live the life of your dreams. To be you 100 percent. To use your gifts to the maximum. Open your mind to the possibility that this is possible. What does the inner voice tell you when you relax and allow yourself to feel your passion? How does it feel?

No. 7
Do the right thing and accept the consequences

> **The number 7 cause of suffering and unhappiness is not doing the right thing because you're afraid of the consequences.**

Step 1:

Are there times in your life when you are not standing up for what you know is right? We can all answer yes to this to a greater or lesser degree. Every one of us is challenged to live honestly and with integrity. Write down as freely and as honestly as you can the times and the situations when you feel you are so afraid of the consequences that you do not do what you think is right. These can be small, rather insignificant incidents in your interpersonal relationships as well as events that take place in the public arena.

Step 2:

Write down and envision doing the right thing in the situations you listed above and seeing and dealing with the consequences you're afraid of. Are the consequences as bad as you think? How will they change your life? And how will you feel about yourself?

No. 8
Deal with what is in front of you and forget the rest

The number 8 cause of suffering and unhappiness is shadowboxing with illusions instead of dealing with the reality in front of you.

Step 1:

Write down as many situations as you can think of where you are sabotaging your ability to act effectively in the present moment because you are distracted by preconceived ideas or stories and don't see what's really going on in front of your eyes. It doesn't matter if the events are big or small; write them all down so you can become more aware of what you are doing.

Step 2:

Write down and envision how you would deal with these situations if you were fully present and focused on what was going on in front of you and could really hear the voice of wisdom inside you speaking clearly, instead of being distracted by preconceived ideas, stories and conditioned responses.

No. 9
Know what is what

> **The number 9 cause of suffering and unhappiness is wanting absolute satisfaction from relative experiences.**

Step 1:

Write down here all the places in your life where you are looking for absolute satisfaction. Are you hoping for absolute satisfaction from your relationship? If so write it down. Or are you looking for absolute satisfaction from your job, your career, your money? Write down everything you can think of where your expectations are out of harmony with reality.

Step 2:

Write down and try to envision how you would relate to these issues and areas if you didn't expect to get absolute satisfaction from them? How would it feel if you allowed things to change naturally? And in what ways would you act and live differently?

No. 10
Learn to see beyond impermanence

> **The number 10 cause of suffering and unhappiness is believing we become nothing.**

Step 1:

Write down here your thoughts about death and dying as honestly as you can. What do you really think about death? Do you believe that death is dangerous? And what about life? Is life dangerous too? Do you believe that something can become nothing? Try to honestly explore your thoughts about these big issues even if it feels uncomfortable. Relax and let go.

Step 2:

Write down and try to envision how it would feel if you really couldn't believe that death is dangerous. How would you live your life if you really felt that you were a part of everything and would always be a part of everything? What would you do differently? Meditate on the concept 'something cannot become nothing'.

Conclusion

The shocking truth about happiness

After all you have been through (in this book and in life), the shocking truth about happiness is that nothing external can make you either happy or unhappy. Only your thoughts about life can do this because it's all happening in you! No outside event, no thing, no circumstance, no person, nothing besides your thoughts can make you happy. This is the way of it; this is the way it works. So…

Dream, play and have a happy life!

Epilogue: Don't believe what you think

> **The absolute main cause of suffering and unhappiness is believing what you think.**

If I had to sum it all up, I'd have to say that the root cause of all our suffering is *believing what we think.* If we didn't believe what we think, it would be impossible to suffer.

If we didn't believe what we think – all that would be left is *what is.* And that would be reality. And reality is not what we think! Reality just is. Reality is beyond explaining – beyond understanding – beyond thought. And even though reality is not something we can conceptualize, reality is something we can *see* – and *experience directly.*

And it's more than that – reality is what we are.

Reality is what is.

But when we believe what we think, instead of just *seeing directly*, it is as if we try to put an artificial matrix of ideas on top of reality – and then we suffer when our matrix and reality don't fit together. We suffer when our thoughts – this artificial matrix – and reality don't match. We suffer when our thoughts and reality turn out to be two different things. And this is *always* the case. Our thoughts and reality are always two different things. Always! Because reality is beyond thought. Reality is beyond understanding. Reality cannot be captured, caught, or explained. Reality just is. And it can only been seen and experienced in each now moment. But reality is not what we think – nor is it what we think it is either!

It's beyond all that. Beyond understanding.

So that is why I say, if you want to live a happy life – *don't believe what you think!*

Book List

Chapter 1:
Sri Nisargadatta Maharaj, *I Am That – Talks with Sri Nisargadatta Maharaj* (Durham, North Carolina, The Acorn Press, 1973)

Chapter 3:
Manuel J. Smith Ph.D, *When I say no, I feel guilty* (New York, Bantam Books, 1975)

Chapter 4:
Byron Katie with Stephen Mitchell, *Loving What Is* (London, Rider, 2002)

Byron Katie with Michael Katz, *I Need Your Love – Is That True?* (London, Rider, 2005)

Chapter 5:
Steve Hagen, *Buddhism plain and simple* (London, Penguin Books, 1997)

Chapter 7:
Thomas Byrom, *The Dhammapada/The Sayings of the Buddha* (New York, Bell Tower, 1976)

M.K. Gandhi, *An Autobiography or The Story of My Experiments with Truth* (London, Penguin Books, 1927)

Richard Attenborough, the film *Gandhi* 1982

Eknath Easwaran, *The Bhagavad Gita* (Callifornia, Nilgiri Press, 1985)

Eknath Easwaran, *Gandhi The Man – The Story of His Transformation* (California, Nilgiri Press, 1972)

Chapter 8:
Sri Nisargadatta Maharaj, *I Am That – Talks with Sri Nisargadatta Maharaj* (Durham, North Carolina, The Acorn Press, 1973)

Thich Nhat Hanh, *No Death, No Fear – Comforting Wisdom for Life* (New York, Riverhead Books, 2002)

About Barbara Berger

Barbara Berger has been a seeker all her life. This book, like all Barbara's other books, is based on her life work which has always been to try to find a way out of suffering. Her quest to ease suffering has led Barbara to explore many different pathways and approaches – mental, physical, metaphysical, psychological and spiritual.

Barbara was born and grew up in the United States. After dropping out of Sarah Lawrence College and leaving the US in the mid-'60s in protest against the Vietnam War, Barbara and her first husband settled in Scandinavia. After two years in Sweden, Barbara moved to Copenhagen, Denmark and married a Dane. There she continued her quest with a passionate interest in the role of food in our mental and physical well-being. When Barbara discovered in the early 1980s that health foods and diet were not enough to ensure true well-being, Barbara began to study the science of the mind, the nature of consciousness, metaphysics, and finally traditional spirituality and psychology. She also left her Danish husband and became a single parent to her three sons.

To date, Barbara has written 15 self-empowerment books documenting and presenting the tools and insights she has discovered over the years on her quest. Her books include the international bestseller *The Road to Power – Fast Food for the Soul* (published in 30 languages), *Are You Happy Now? 10 Ways to Live a Happy Life* (published in 15 languages), *The Awakening Human Being – A Guide to the Power of Mind*, and *Sane Self Talk – Cultivating the Voice of Sanity Within*. In all her books, Barbara explores and explains the incredible power of mind and how we can use this power wisely to live happy lives right now, regardless of outer events and circumstances. Barbara also gives lectures and workshops (with her eldest son and author Tim Ray) and offers private sessions to individuals who wish to work intensely with her. Barbara lives and works in Copenhagen, Denmark.

For more about Barbara Berger, see: www.beamteam.com

BOOKS

O is a symbol of the world, of oneness and unity. In different cultures it also means the "eye," symbolizing knowledge and insight. We aim to publish books that are accessible, constructive and that challenge accepted opinion, both that of academia and the "moral majority."

Our books are available in all good English language bookstores worldwide. If you don't see the book on the shelves ask the bookstore to order it for you, quoting the ISBN number and title. Alternatively you can order online (all major online retail sites carry our titles) or contact the distributor in the relevant country, listed on the copyright page.

See our website **www.o-books.net** for a full list of over 500 titles, growing by 100 a year.

And tune in to myspiritradio.com for our book review radio show, hosted by June-Elleni Laine, where you can listen to the authors discussing their books.

MySpiritRadio